Yankee Folk Crafts

YANKEE FOLK CRAFTS

CREATE YOUR OWN country-style heirlooms with project designs and instructions for stenciling, paper cutting, wood carving, antiquing, and much more . . . .

by Carole Yeager

A division of Yankee Publishing Incorporated
Dublin, New Hampshire

To Amanda and Brian —
the very best part of life.

Designed and illustrated by
Jill Shaffer
Art Assistants: Maryann Mattson
and Susan Dunholter

Yankee Publishing Incorporated
Dublin, New Hampshire 03444

First Edition

Library of Congress Cataloging-in-Publication Data

Yeager, Carole, 1949—
  Yankee folk crafts.

  Source guide: p.
  Bibliography: p.
  1. Handicraft—United States.   I. Title.
TT23.Y43   1988   745   88-10781
ISBN 0-89909-164-4

Acknowledgments

It wouldn't have been possible without you . . .

To Mandy and Brian for understanding each time they heard "Can we do it later?"

To my husband John, a constant source of encouragement and help, who, through his dogged persistence, introduced me (or should I say, dragged me) into the twentieth century — and the World of the Word Processor.

To Meredith Bernstein, my friend and agent, for making that first phone call.

To Jill Mason, my editor, for her patience and commitment to perfection.

To my Mom and Dad Garrahan, who would have been proud.

To Mom and Dad Yeager for their support and for always being there when Mandy and Brian needed their loving grandparents in a hurry!

To my many friends and relatives who were there with time, encouragement, and a kind word when I needed it.

To Lawrence and Jack Yeager for all their time and effort in drafting the exploded drawings, and to Michele Kelly for her calligraphy.

To the staff of Yankee Publishing for putting it all together.

To my four-legged friends Misty the cat and Dandy our Springer for warming my feet and keeping me company on many 3:00 A.M. mornings when it seemed the whole world had gone to bed.

And last, but not least, to the countless known, unknown, and often uncelebrated craftspeople from the past and present whose work serves as a constant source of joy and inspiration.

Contents

"All items that are made by hand have a special mystique about them. They represent to us a bond with their maker, known or unknown. It gives us respect, if not love for the effort that was put forth. Whenever we make something with our hands, no matter how refined or crude, we give of ourselves."

– Author Unknown

Introduction

IN THIS technologically advanced and sometimes impersonal twentieth century, an unquestionable phenomenon is occurring in homes across the country. Although it is most often associated with a style of decorating, what's changing is more than just a look: it reflects a way of life, the warmth of family and friends, the charm of handcrafted objects, and an appreciation for the simple, unpretentious attitudes of the past. Because they represent a state of mind more than any place, stenciled walls, country furniture, and folk art of any kind are as at home in a Manhattan condominium as in a New England farmhouse.

This trend is due, in part, to a desire to return to a more tranquil, nostalgic life style, to a time when the world seemed less hurried, more innocent. The feeling can be evoked, linking today's rooms with the past, by the use and display of carefully chosen antiques, collectibles, and handcrafts — gentle reminders of another time. Since so many of us are charmed by folk-art pieces of the past, however, the increased demand has caused a corresponding increase in prices, making it virtually impossible to own the collectibles we admire. In some ways, our dilemma can be compared to that confronting many of America's earliest settlers. They, too, often lacked the resources to obtain that which they coveted. Their new homes were often stark, lacking many comforts, from household goods to playthings for the children. But their needs served as a catalyst for their resourcefulness; for, more important than tangible goods, they brought with them individual talents, ideas, and an unabashed spirit of creativity. Unencumbered by ideas of what they could not do, they created, capturing bits of time as seen through the eyes of often self-taught craftspeople. These industrious men and women left behind a legacy of creativity, ingenuity, and a delightfully uninhibited sense of design — American folk art.

This book is designed for those wanting to rediscover the joy and satisfaction of working with one's hands. Its pages are filled with charming ideas for creating homespun folk-art-style heirlooms from wood, fabric, paper, and more. You'll find projects for every member of the family, to be used in every room of your home, from vintage-style toys to "folk-heart" furniture. Some projects are copied from existing American folk art, while others are updated versions of old ideas. In every case, instructions are simplified so that even a first-time do-it-yourselfer can turn out instant family treasures. If you are a beginner, Chapter 1 will help familiarize you with the supplies, tools, and techniques to get started. Don't be overly concerned about perfection — just enjoy the process of creating. Somehow it always seems that, magically, the more you enjoy doing something, the better the results! An added bonus is that for every person who makes one of the projects, there will likely be at least a dozen others who will enjoy receiving or just looking at it.

I hope this book succeeds in unlocking that indigenous spirit of creativity that lives in each and every one of you — and along the way may you discover a hidden talent or satisfying hobby.

1
The Basics

THE INFORMATION contained in this chapter covers some of the basic knowledge and skills required to complete the projects in this book. Although making mistakes has always been a natural part of my learning experiences, taking some time now to review this section will enable your work to progress more smoothly later.

Paints

All the painted projects in this book, unless otherwise noted, are painted with water-based acrylic paints. Acrylics are fast drying, water soluble, and excellent for painting on paper, wood, and fabric. Since acrylics dry quickly, place only a small amount of paint on your palette at a time (use a paper plate or a disposable paper palette). It's a good idea to keep an atomizer of water nearby for misting and freshening the paint. Extender can be added to acrylics to slow the drying time. (It is also used for blending and thinning the paint without changing the paint's consistency as mixing with water does.)

For most projects, I have listed suggested colors of paint. For simplification, the color names I use are usually Folk Art by Plaid brand paints; however, any of the other popular brands (Ceramcoat by Delta or Country Colors by Illinois Bronze, for example) will work equally well. The color conversion chart on page 11 lists generic colors for all the Folk Art paints used in this book. Paints are available in myriad colors and come packaged in one-ounce jars, two-ounce squeeze bottles, and, for larger projects, eight-ounce cans. Remember that the colors listed for each project are only suggestions; I encourage you to experiment and be creative with your colors.

For centuries, skimmed milk or buttermilk was combined with natural colorants (earth clays) and lime to produce unrefined, homemade paint. When used on wood, this "milk paint" produced a flat, dusty color with a somewhat grainy appearance. You can re-create this authentic, centuries-old look by using commercially prepared powdered milk paint (see the Source Guide on page 159). This folk-art finish is especially suited to the furniture projects in this book. But be forewarned: The adhesion to wood is so good that you won't be able to strip the paint off once it has dried.

A wash is another effective technique used to achieve a worn, aged appearance. A mixture of 1 part paint to 3–4 parts water will produce a thin transparency of color.

COLOR CONVERSION CHART
Folk Art Colors to Generic Colors

Apricot Cream — peach
Bluebell — light blue
Burgundy — dark red
Buttercup — medium yellow
Calico Red — bright red
Cherokee Rose — dusty pink
Cinnamon — pale orange
Clover — medium yellow-green
Coastal Blue — bright sky blue
Coffee Bean — medium brown
Dove Gray — pale gray
Harvest Gold — golden yellow
Honey Comb — tan
Lemonade — pale yellow
Nutmeg — yellow-brown
Paisley Blue — bright blue
Patchwork Green — medium green
Raspberry Wine — deep red
Red Clay — brownish red
Rusty Nail — brownish orange
Shamrock — medium green
Skintone — pink flesh
Slate Blue — dark gray-blue
Taffy — off-white
Thicket — black-green
Wrought Iron — gray-black

Brushes

The following paragraphs contain descriptions of the various types of brushes used for the painted projects in this book (stencil brushes are discussed separately in Chapter 4). Using the right brush for a particular project will make a noticeable difference in the ease of painting and in the results. Always buy the best-quality brush you can afford.

A brush is made from either a synthetic material (nylon or taklon) or a natural material (for example, bristle brushes are made of hog hair and sable brushes of weasel hair). Bristle brushes are quite coarse and are good to use when working with thicker paints (acrylics and oils), for feathering and dry-brushing, or for texturing. Sable brushes are softer and are well suited to detail painting with thinner paint (watercolors and thinned acrylics). Synthetic brushes are generally less expensive than their counterparts made from natural hair, and, unless otherwise noted, they can be used for any of the projects in this book.

The basic types of brushes used in this book are shown in Figure 1-1. The first three brushes, A, B, and C, are available in both natural and synthetic hair. The brush heads range from very fine to very thick and are sized by number; the lower the number, the smaller the brush. Occasionally, a specific size, shape, and hair type is called for in a project's supply list.

Flats (A): Flats are square-ended, long-bristle brushes. Broad strokes can be made with the flat edge, and fine lines can be made with the side of the bristles, making this a very versatile brush and an excellent choice for most of the painted projects in this book.

Brights (B): Brights are square-ended, short-bristle brushes, similar to a flat brush but offering more control in detail work. They are especially suited to working with thicker paint.

Rounds (C): Rounds are rounded brushes with tapered, pointed ends. The shape is ideal for detail painting, painting fine lines, and applying thin paint.

Sponge brushes (D): Sponge brushes are disposable brushes made from a synthetic polyfoam material. They can be reused several times. They leave little or no stroke mark and are ideal for staining, sealing, basecoating, painting, and spreading glue, but they are not recommended for spreading lacquer or varnish. They are available in widths ranging from 1" to 4".

Whatever brush you use, make sure you thoroughly clean it after each use; any paint left at the edge of the ferrule (the metal portion of the brush, which holds the bristles) will harden and cause the brush hairs to become splayed. After cleaning, form the brush into its original shape and store it vertically, resting on its handle.

FIG. 1-1. *Types of brushes.*

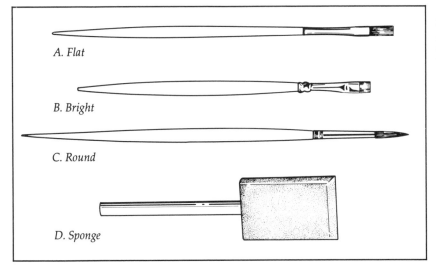

A. Flat

B. Bright

C. Round

D. Sponge

Patterns and Designs

To copy a pattern: First place a piece of tracing paper over the design you wish to copy. Hold the paper in place with paper clips or small pieces of tape (transparent or masking). Using a sharp pencil, trace around the outline of the design. Another method of copying (and enlarging) patterns is to use a photocopy machine. The availability of a machine and the cost involved will determine the practicality of this method. Note, however, that copiers might not copy or enlarge uniformly in both directions, making this a questionable method for projects involving assembly of pieces for which an exact fit is required.

To transfer a pattern: Once you have copied your design onto tracing paper, cut out an equal-size piece of graphite paper. (If you are using a new piece of graphite paper, it's a good idea to remove some of the graphite by wiping it with a paper towel. New graphite often leaves smudges on the surface or transfers lines that are too dark.) Sandwich the graphite paper (shiny side down) between the tracing paper and the surface to which you are transferring the design. Hold the paper in place with tape and, using a sharp pencil, an empty ballpoint pen, or a stylus, lightly trace the design. Don't press too hard on the pencil or stylus, as you don't want to leave an indentation on the surface. You can remove any unwanted traces of graphite with an eraser.

If you want to transfer a very small pattern design (the cat or doll faces in Chapter 5, for example) and can't justify buying a full sheet or box of graphite paper, you can make your own transfer paper. Just trace the pattern onto tracing paper, then coat the other side with lead from a pencil; turn the paper over and trace to transfer your pattern.

To enlarge a pattern: Whenever possible, the patterns in this book are given full size or as a half pattern to eliminate the need to enlarge. When it is necessary to enlarge a pattern (the angel weather vane in Chapter 7 and the child's settle bench in Chapter 8), use the grid on which the pattern is drawn to plot a sufficient number of points to allow a free-hand drawing of the full-size pattern. To begin, count the number of vertical and horizontal squares used on the grid and apply the scale to determine what size paper is needed for the full-size pattern. (Poster board works well for making patterns.)

Select two adjacent edges of this paper (for example, the left edge and the bottom) to serve as axes from which points are measured. Select a point on the pattern line that is at a grid line intersection, count the number of squares up from the horizontal axis and the number of squares over from the vertical axis, apply the scale, and plot these measurements on the full-size pattern. Use a framing square to ensure that the points you are plotting are positioned accurately. Now follow the pattern line to the next intersection, count the vertical and horizontal squares, and plot this point on your pattern. Continue until all grid intersection points have been plotted, or until you have plotted enough points to draw the pattern. Cut out the pattern and trace it onto the wood or other material you are using.

To find the center point: When you must find the exact center point of a square or rectangular object (such as a floorcloth or pillow top), use this easy and accurate method. (See Figure 1-2.) Using a yardstick, draw a straight line to join two opposite corners; then draw another straight line to join the remaining two corners. The point at which these lines intersect is the exact center point.

FIG. 1-2. *Finding the center of a square or rectangle.*

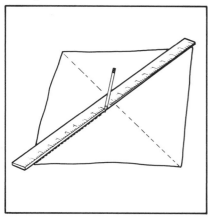

Hand Tools

Following is a list and description of the hand tools used for the various wood projects in this book. Always buy the best quality you can afford; shoddy tools can break, causing injury to you or your project. Good tools are not cheap, but when properly cared for, they last a lifetime and are worth the investment. It's not necessary to own every tool listed here, but do try to use the right tool for the job. This goes for power tools, too.

C-clamp: C-clamps are used to apply pressure to two surfaces from opposite directions. A 4"–6" clamp is a good all-purpose size and is sufficient for all the projects in this book. Clamps are used to hold pieces of wood together to ensure a tight glue bond and to secure boards to a bench, sawhorse, or other stable support while cutting with a saber saw.

Coping saw: A coping saw is used for cutting intricate patterns in thin wood. Its thin blade is held tightly between two lugs, one in the handle and the other in the frame. The blade is able to rotate a full 360 degrees and cut up to 5" from the edge of the board. Its recommended use in this book is to make gross cuts from carving blocks in Chapter 7.

Crosscut saw: The crosscut saw is the familiar handsaw used for cutting across the grain of a piece of wood. If you are buying a new one, look for one with eight teeth (or points) to the inch. If you already have one, make sure it is sharp and has the proper set to its teeth for best performance. If needed, have the saw sharpened and set. A crosscut saw can be used on the straight cuts of the furniture projects in Chapter 8; if you are skilled in its use, it will provide a straighter cut than the saber saw.

Glue: Using the right type of glue on a project will help ensure the best results. The main types of glue used in this book are:

• *quick-drying glue* — a good, all-purpose, water-based glue that dries fast and clear (Elmer's Glue-All, for example). Use it on paper and other porous materials.

• *tacky glue* — an extra thick white glue (Aleene's "Tacky" Glue, for example). Use it when a faster drying time is needed, as on the lampshades.

• *wood glue* — a water-based glue that penetrates wood deeply for a strong bond (Elmer's Carpenter's Wood Glue, for example).

• *hide glue* — an animal-based glue product (Franklin Hide Glue, for example), used to create a crackle finish on the gameboards (Chapter 6) and the weather vane (Chapter 7). Hide glue can also be used for the furniture projects. It is available in most hardware or home stores.

• *hot-glue gun* — an electric gun activated by pulling a trigger to apply molten hot glue. It bonds almost anything to anything in seconds, but use care when operating since the glue will stick to and burn fingers.

Hammer: The hammer used in these projects is a standard claw hammer. Any claw hammer designed for nailing wood is sufficient, but its quality will greatly affect its ease of use. Buy a medium-weight quality hammer and save yourself the aggravation.

Long-nose pliers: Long-nose pliers are well suited to holding small nails while you are hammering. This is particularly helpful when assembling the wagon in Chapter 5, where it is necessary to hold and drive ½" brads. A good size for general use is 7". Long-nose pliers also have a wire cutter built into their jaws, which can be used to cut nails (Chapter 5, Express Wagon).

Miter box: A miter box is used to provide precise alignment of narrow pieces of wood in order to make exact angle cuts. It also can be used to make exact 90-degree cuts. You can make some of the cuts required for projects in this book (especially for the dowels for the quilt rack in Chapter 8) more accurately using this tool.

Nail set: This tool is used to recess nail heads below the surface of the wood. You can then achieve a more finished look by filling the holes with wood filler. Nail sets come with different-size tips to accommodate various-size nails. You can use a larger nail (especially a hard-cut nail) to recess the smaller nail instead, but this method might require some practice.

Planes: Planes are used to remove a controlled amount of wood, using a shaving action. There are numerous varieties, each with a specific purpose. The type most suited to the requirements in the Chapter 8 furniture projects is the block plane, which is used for relatively small pieces of wood. It can be held in one hand and is one of the least expensive planes. While primarily designed for cross-grain planing, it also can be used for planing with the grain. An even better variation of this tool is the Surform design made by Stanley. The Surform has a replaceable planing surface made up of numerous cutting ridges that take off many hairlike shavings of wood at once.

Rasp: A rasp is a coarse file used to shape wood. It is used to round edges more quickly than can be done with sandpaper. After rasping, you should always sand the surface smooth.

Screwdrivers: Screwdrivers come in various types, shapes, and sizes. For the projects in this book, you should have a small and a medium-size flat-tipped screwdriver.

Square: There are many types of squares, but the most versatile is a carpenter's framing square. A combination square — one that can also make a 45-degree angle — is easier to use for smaller pieces of wood. Both are helpful, but if you plan to purchase only one, it should be the framing square.

Steel tape ruler: A steel tape measure, as it is also called, is a valuable tool for measuring distances. It is fast, accurate, and easy to carry. A 12' tape is a good all-purpose size, although a 6' tape is sufficient for the projects in this book.

Tack cloth: A tack cloth is a piece of cheesecloth that has been treated with varnish and turpentine. Use it to remove dust particles from wood before you apply a finish. It is inexpensive and available at most hardware stores or home centers.

X-acto knives: Two different X-acto knives are referred to in this book. In Chapter 7 an X-acto *carving* knife is described (see page 123). Every other mention of an X-acto knife in these pages refers to a No. 1 X-acto knife, a versatile *all-purpose* knife pictured in color plate 6. Use it with a No. 11 blade.

Power Tools

Whether or not you have experience using power tools, you should have a healthy respect for them but should not be intimidated by them. Work goes faster when electric power replaces human effort, and the result is often better because a power tool has precise controls. I was first introduced to power tools several Christmases ago when I found two very large packages addressed to me under our tree. Much to my surprise, they turned out to contain a scroll saw and a band saw. At that time, I was very interested in painting on wood, but my creativity was stymied when I couldn't find the wood cutouts I wanted. These saws proved to be the perfect solution. With some instruction from my ever-patient husband and a little practice, I was soon cutting out all sorts of one-of-a-kind shapes whenever the inspiration or need arose.

When using any kind of power tool (especially saws), it's important to *read all the instructions carefully*. If possible, have the tool demonstrated before purchasing it, so you can observe its operation and have all your questions answered. If this is not possible, have someone with experience work with you until you understand and feel comfortable using it.

Always work in a well-lighted area, always wear safety goggles to protect your eyes from flying debris, and *never* leave a tool running and unattended. Never wear loose clothing, and always tie back long hair. Be sure your drill bits and saw blades are sharp. Worn bits or blades will perform poorly and might stick, causing a drill or saw to jerk out of control. If you maintain your tools properly, you're sure to be rewarded with years of problem-free service.

Band saw: Although relatively expensive ($100 plus), and optional for the projects in this book, the band saw is a very versatile power tool. It is available in two- and three-wheel types. It does well with both straight and curved cuts and a radius of about 1″ or greater, and it can make end cuts at angles from 0 to 60 degrees. It generally has a throat of 10″ to 12″ and can cut pieces up to 2½″ to 6″ depending on the type and model. *Use extreme care!* Just as it makes short work of the furniture projects in Chapter 8, it can make short work of your fingers.

Blades for this saw come in the form of a continuous band (hence the name) in various lengths, widths, and tooth ratings. Lengths are matched to the particular saw. Widths are selected for the type of cut to be made — narrow blades for scroll work, wide blades for straight cuts, and medium blades for general purpose work. The coarseness is rated in teeth per inch: the fewer teeth, the coarser the blade. A coarse blade (four teeth per inch) is used for thick wood or rough, fast cuts in common wood thicknesses. A greater number of teeth is used for finer cuts, thinner wood, or even for cutting metals. The most practical blade for the projects in this book is medium width, six teeth per inch. A supplier is listed in the Source Guide on page 159.

Counterbore bit: I suggest that if you do not own a set of these bits, you get one on your next trip to the store. They come in sets of four — No. 6, No. 8, No. 10, and No. 12. For projects that require numerous holes for screws, they work like magic. Each bit is a standard drill bit surrounded by a collar that can be adjusted to control the depth of the drill hole. The combination of this bit and collar allows you to bore both pilot and shank holes and countersinks or counterbores — all in one operation.

Color plate 1, above: Angel and Heart Scherenschnitte Birth Announcement (Chapter 2); Sheep Pull Toy, Wooden Folk Dolls, and Express Wagon (Chapter 5); Uncle Sam Whirligig (Chapter 7); Sun and Moon Checkerboard (Chapter 6). **Color plate 2, left:** Stenciled Kitten Shade and Noah's Ark Scherenschnitte (Chapter 2); Cornhusk Dolls (Chapter 3); Chunky Blocks (Chapter 5).

Color plate 3, left: Angel and Heart Scherenschnitte Birth Announcement (Chapter 2); Herb Wreath (Chapter 3); The Basic Checkerboard (Chapter 6); Trestle Table and Country Benches (Chapter 8). **Color plate 4, above:** Summer's Bounty Painted Shade and House with Willows Scherenschnitte (Chapter 2); Angel Weather Vane and Lesser Yellowlegs Decoy (Chapter 7); Parcheesi Board (Chapter 6).

Color plate 5, above: Dried Apple Wreath with
Cinnamon Hearts and Harvest Wreath (Chapter 3);
Flowers and Vines Checkerboard (Chapter 6).
Color plate 6, right *(clockwise from top left):* Potato
Prints, Scratched-Carved Eggs, Apple Jack-o'-
Lantern (Chapter 3); Tabletop Tree Ornament
(Chapter 2); Spicy Cookie Ornaments and Spicy
Fruit Pomander Balls (Chapter 3).

Color plate 7, left: Quilt Rack and Child's Settle Bench (Chapter 8); Stenciled Tulip Pillow and Stenciled Floorcloth (Chapter 4); Wooden Folk Dolls and Sheep Pull Toy (Chapter 5). **Color plate 8, above:** Painted Welcome Board (Chapter 4); Decorated Straw Hat (Chapter 3).

Color plate 9, above: Cut and Pierced Heart Shade (Chapter 2); Mini Potpourri Wreath (Chapter 3); Birds in the Nest Scherenschnitte and Bandboxes (Chapter 2); Captivating Kittens (Chapter 5); Double Hearts Checkerboard (Chapter 6).
Color plate 10, right: Cut and Pierced Pineapple Shade and Love Birds Scherenschnitte (Chapter 2); Pomander Ball (Chapter 3).

Electric drill: Electric drills come in a wide range of types and quality levels and are used mainly to make holes in wood. For all-around home use, choose a variable-speed drill that is also reversible. It should have a locking mechanism for the trigger and a ⅜″ capacity chuck. Drill bits are affixed to the drill by means of the chuck, a three-point clamping mechanism that is tightened (and loosened) with a geared key. The drill is generally a safe tool to use, but remember to tie back long hair and avoid loose-fitting clothing.

Saber saw (jigsaw): The saber saw is an extremely useful tool capable of crosscutting, ripping, sawing curves, beveling, and starting a cut in the middle of a board. All the cuts in the furniture projects in Chapter 8 can be made using this saw. Choose one that has a variable speed, cuts bevels, and blows the sawdust away from the cutting line. Its interchangeable blades can be matched to a variety of materials and thicknesses: for the furniture projects, choose a narrow ten- or twelve-tooth (per inch) blade; for the toy projects (Chapter 5), a wide fourteen-tooth blade.

Sander: Using an electric sander sure beats hand-sanding! Either a palm sander or an orbital sander will suffice for the projects in this book. Don't use any sander for rounding corners, though: a sharp corner can quickly and easily poke through the sandpaper and permanently damage the foam base. Also, do not use a belt sander for any of the projects in this book; it is designed for large jobs and would be too difficult to control.

Scroll saw: A stationary tabletop saw, with a thin, flexible blade, the scroll saw is excellent for intricate work in thin wood. Because the teeth of the blades are very small, this saw does not pose the same threat to misplaced fingers that some other power saws do. Even so, be cautious: it has the ability to inflict cuts in fingers as easily as in wood. This tool is optional for the projects in this book.

Wood Selection

All the wood projects in this book are made from white (Ponderosa) pine, unless otherwise noted. The advantages of using pine are many: It is inexpensive, easy to find, and easy to cut, carve, saw, and nail. It is neutral in color and, when stained, can mimic the appearance of many woods. It has an attractive grain, and it accepts many types of finishes. Even the primary disadvantage — that it dents easily — becomes an advantage with the projects in this book, as their appearance is enhanced by an aged look.

What about using hardwoods? Although you can use hardwoods, they are exceedingly more difficult to work with. More precise tools are needed, and screws should be substituted for nails. The primary consideration in using hardwoods, however, is the expense, which is many times greater than for pine.

Dimensions: The wood used for the projects in this book is of standard dimensions. Most measurements of standard-dimension lumber reflect the rough-cut dimensions, however, and might at first be somewhat misleading. The boards that you buy from a lumberyard or home center have been planed. Thus, the actual (planed) measurements are considerably less than the named (nominal) measurements. For example, a 1" x 12" board would have been planed on both the sides and edges, and the planed dimensions would be approximately ¾" by 11¼". There will be slight variations in the planed dimensions, however, especially in the width. The nominal, or pre-planed, dimensions are given for all the projects in this book.

The order of the dimensions given is always the same: thickness x width x length. All the projects in this book adhere to this format except where I have specified the length first, for example, a 10" length of 1" (thickness) x 6" (width).

It should be noted that apart from the planed width variations, differences in width will occur with the expansion and contraction of the wood itself. It is a good idea, therefore, to acclimate the wood to the area in which the finished piece will be used before you begin the project. This allows the wood to expand or shrink (across the grain only) to the size that will be normal for the usage area. For example, if you store the boards for the trestle table project in Chapter 8 in an area of high humidity (perhaps a basement), assemble it there, and then move it to the kitchen, the boards in the tabletop might shrink and leave gaps between them. It should take a week or more to condition the wood to the humidity level of the usage area.

Grading: Pine is graded according to the clarity of the boards. The most common defect in lumber is the presence of knots, but also considered in the grade determination is the presence of pitch, pith (the spongy center of a log), splits, and bark. A No. 1 board is considered defect-free, while a No. 2 board has some defects, usually knots. A No. 3 board has many defects and is not suitable for the projects in this book. It is not necessary to purchase only top-grade lumber; if chosen carefully, No. 2 lumber will serve well for most of the projects in this book. But be certain that what you do buy is well seasoned and dry. This will prevent shrinking, warping, or splitting later on. Especially avoid pieces with *dead knots*, dense orange spots with a dark brown ring around them (actually from a dead branch around which the tree has grown). As these knots shrink with age, they are likely to fall out. Look for pieces that have no traces of pitch (resin), as it would have to be removed — with great difficulty — before finishing.

Grain: Grain refers to the fibers of the wood. It is important to pay attention to the direction of the grain when laying out your wood projects because it determines the strength of the finished product. In general, the grain should run in the direction of the longest dimension. For example, for the kitten project in Chapter 5, the grain should be parallel to the lengths of both the legs and the tail. If the grain was perpendicular, these pieces could be easily broken.

Knots: As mentioned previously, knots detract from the value of a piece of wood. On some projects, however, the presence of knots is a desirable characteristic, adding a rustic appearance to the piece. While the use of lumber with knots is acceptable, improper placement of knots within the piece is . . . not. Remember that, because of its density, the knot is brittle; it cannot be satisfactorily nailed, and its presence in narrow pieces of wood could compromise the strength of the project. Use care in layout and make sure you check both sides of the wood — knots often run at unusual angles. Finally, don't lay out pieces so that you will have to saw directly through a knot, especially a dead one, as it might eventually crack or fall out.

Woodworking Tips

Countersinking: Countersinking is a technique used to hide nail or screw heads by driving them flush with or below the surface of the wood, resulting in a more finished look.

To countersink a nail head, place a nail set or a larger nail over the head you wish to hide and strike it with a hammer, recessing the head slightly ($\frac{1}{16}$" to $\frac{1}{8}$") below the surface. Fill the hole with wood putty or filler, allow it to dry, and sand it flush with the surface. Paint or stain the piece to finish it.

To countersink a screw head, use a countersink or counterbore bit (see page 16) to bore a bevel into the top of the hole to a depth equal to the size of the screw head. This will allow it to be driven flush with the surface.

Counterboring screw holes: When using flat-head screws, it is often desirable to conceal the heads. This is done with a counterbore bit, which places the head of the screw far enough below the surface so that you can either fill the remaining hole with putty or spackling, plug it with a decorative wooden cap, or disguise it with a flush-sanded wooden screw-hole plug. Use the cap or plug required for the size screw you are using and tap it in place (with a small amount of glue if necessary).

Sanding: For the wood projects in this book, use either garnet, aluminum oxide, or silicon carbide sandpaper. These types are designed specifically for wood and are available in extra-fine to extra-coarse grits. Whether you are using an electric sander or sanding by hand, start with a coarse grit (if the surface is very rough) and finish with a fine grit, always sanding *with* the grain. Sanding across the grain will leave hard-to-remove scratches on the wood. When hand-sanding a large, flat surface, it is easier and more efficient to use a sanding block. You can make your own by wrapping a piece of sponge rubber or an old towel around a block of wood (this provides resiliency), then wrapping the sandpaper around both and securing it to the block with thumbtacks. After sanding, always wipe the wood with a tack cloth to remove all the sawdust before going on to the next finishing step. For more information on sanding, see Power Tools–Sander, page 17.

Sealing wood: Sealing is an optional step. If I want a weathered and worn look, I skip the sealer and paint directly on the raw wood. Sealer is not necessary for the furniture projects in Chapter 8 if you use stain; I don't recommend sealing wood that is to be stained. But for a smoother, more finished painting surface (for the welcome board in Chapter 4 or the wooden dolls in Chapter 5), sealer is essential. A sealer helps to hide flaws and knots and prevents such imperfections from bleeding through your finished project. It also prevents the paint from soaking into the wood, thereby requiring less base coat and ensuring a more even distribution of the color. Use a commercial sealer or make your own: a half-and-half mixture of shellac and denatured alcohol. Apply one or two thin coats to the wood with a brush. Since sealer tends to raise the grain slightly, sand lightly and wipe with a tack cloth between coats and before painting. The sealer will dry very quickly, enabling you to get on with your painting. Wash your brush in household ammonia.

Staining: After sanding, your wood projects are ready to be painted or stained. Stains are available in myriad shades. Do not, however, assume that the color on the lid or label indicates the exact shade of the stain on your project. The finished tone is influenced by the type of wood you are using, so you should always test the stain on the underside of your project or on a piece of scrap wood.

Mix the stain thoroughly before use. Then apply it with a soft cloth or brush (or sponge brush) in thick, even coats, using long strokes. Always apply stain *with* the grain of the wood. When you are finished with a surface, wipe it with a soft cloth to work the stain into the pores of the wood and to remove any excess. If you find that the stain is getting too dark, you can lighten it by wiping the surface with a rag dipped in mineral spirits or turpentine.

Varnishing: Satin-finish clear polyurethane varnish can be used as a final finish on the furniture projects in Chapter 8. (It's also used as a protective finish on the floorcloth in Chapter 4.) It is best to do varnishing in a dust-free room and on a clear day (with an ambient temperature of about 70 degrees). Avoid varnishing on a hot, humid, or rainy day, as the varnish will not dry properly. Stir the varnish slowly but thoroughly (shaking will generate bubbles). Pour a small amount into a separate container and load the lower third or half of your brush with varnish. Use a wide bristle brush or one made specifically for varnish. Begin with long, even, back-and-forth strokes going with the grain, filling in a section that can be covered by the amount of varnish on the brush. Always brush from the surface off the edge rather than from the edge to the center; this prevents runs, as the edge will strip the brush of its load of varnish. Fill in any spots you might have missed with short, across-the-grain strokes. Complete the section by making light, smoothing strokes in one direction, from the leading edge of varnish toward the previously completed section. Work carefully but quickly, trying always to keep a "wet" leading edge. Use the reflection of light on the varnish to find and correct any missed spots while the varnish is still wet. Allow at least twenty-four hours of drying time. If you want additional coats, sand the dried surface lightly with very fine sandpaper between applications, wipe with a tack cloth, and then repeat the process.

Antiquing

Antiquing will give your newly made wood projects a mellow, time-worn appearance. It can be accomplished in the following ways.

Antiquing glaze: By rubbing an antiquing glaze over your finished project, you can tone down the colors and simulate a patina of age. A glaze tends to deepen the colors of the base coat, making them appear richer. Before applying a glaze, spray the project with a matte acrylic sealer. This sealer will prevent the paint from being rubbed off in the antiquing process. (This step isn't necessary for furniture projects. The pieces are too big to spray, and if any paint is rubbed off, the aged look will only be enhanced.)

Purchase a prepared antiquing mix or mix your own glaze by blending equal parts of oil paint and turpentine. The color of oil paint you choose will determine the shade and tone of the antiquing medium. For a rich, warm glaze, mix equal parts of burnt umber *or* raw umber oil paint and turpentine. For a lighter, honey-colored glaze, mix raw umber *or* raw sienna oil paint and turpentine. Either is an excellent all-purpose glaze and will produce an attractive patina over most base colors. Over a blue base coat, however, these glazes tend to leave a dull brown or slightly greenish tinge. To obtain a warm gray patina while retaining a true blue, add a small amount of black paint to either umber glaze. Wear rubber gloves to protect your hands and blend the glaze in a disposable tin pie plate until the mixture is the consistency of light cream (thinner for a lighter glaze).

Dip a soft, lint-free cloth (or a sponge brush) into the antiquing glaze and, starting from the edges and working toward the center, apply the glaze to your project. Work the glaze into corners and depressions. With a clean cloth (cheesecloth works well), gently rub the surface to remove some of the antiquing, leaving dark tones in cracks and corners. (The edges are usually darker than the center.) It is really a matter of taste as to how aged you want your project to look. If your piece gets too dark, lift off some of the glaze by wiping it with a cloth dampened with turpentine. If you want to darken the glaze or produce more shading around the edges, dip a corner of the cloth in straight oil paint, apply it around the edges in a circular motion, and blend it in.

Antiquing cast-metal wheels: To remove the shine from the cast-metal wheels used for the pull toy and wagon in Chapter 5, apply a brass/pewter darkener (the gray patina used in the antiquing of stained glass joints is the same chemical). This product can be found in most full-line craft stores. (See the Source Guide, page 159.) Since this product is quite harsh, use rubber gloves when working with it. Use a small, stiff brush to coat each wheel evenly; work the darkener in between the spokes and touch up light sections as needed. When a wheel is thoroughly covered, rinse it with water and dry it with a paper towel. Be sure to remove any excess chemical, as it tends to turn reddish brown if allowed to dry on the wheels. This chemical is poisonous, so make sure you store it appropriately.

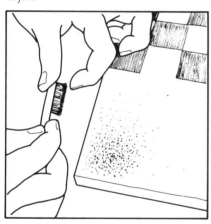

FIG. 1-3. *Hold the brush about 8″ above the object.*

Distressing: Distressing will help remove that just-made look from furniture and other wood projects. Sanding with a fine-grit sandpaper or No. 0 steel wool is one method. Try to imagine which areas would have received the most use if the piece was an antique. Then gently sand the surfaces and round the edges. Gentle sanding can be done after you have painted your project, but if you are doing heavy sanding, do it before staining or painting. Then sand again lightly after painting to remove some of the paint.

You can also simulate the effects of age by hitting the object with a chain, keys, or a bunch of nails held together with a rubber band (children love helping with this). I prefer to use this technique before painting or staining a piece.

Spattering: Spattering is the final step after antiquing and distressing. To get started, you need a stiff-bristled brush (an old toothbrush works well), rubber gloves to protect your hands, newspapers to spread under your project, and your antiquing glaze or thinned (but not watery) black acrylic paint. Dip the ends of the bristles into the glaze or paint. Hold the brush perpendicular to and about 8″ above your project and flick the bristles with your forefinger to spatter your project with a fine, even spray (no blobs or drips). (See Figure 1-3.) To control the size of the speckles, move the brush closer to or farther from the surface. If you are not satisfied with the results, blot it with a paper towel and start again.

2
Paper Artistry

FOR CENTURIES, paper has served as an inspiration for artists. Perhaps because almost anyone could afford a piece of paper, it has always been a favored material for the folk artist. Throughout history, women in particular have enjoyed working with paper. In this medium they are on equal ground with their male counterparts; physical strength is of no value in creating a beautiful piece of art from paper. Paper was, and still is, a medium in which the quality of the product is determined by neatness and the artist's imagination.

The early craftspeople who worked with paper made their contribution to the world of art in many different ways. Intricate paper cuttings, origami, bandboxes, silhouettes, and frakturs are just a few examples of their artistry. Alas, since paper is such a perishable material, many of these treasures have been lost forever. Fortunately, however, the techniques used to create them have survived and are once again being practiced.

This chapter provides easy-to-follow instructions and patterns that will allow you to re-create beautiful forms of folk art. All you need is some patience, a little practice, and a minimum of supplies. Your reward will be not only in the creation of these beautiful crafts, but also in the knowledge that you are a part of that new generation of craftspeople helping to preserve a part of our common heritage.

Bandboxes

SUPPLIES
Newspaper (preferably old) or
  wrapping paper for lining
1 yard of wallpaper
22" x 28" piece of medium-weight
  cardboard, artist's show card,
  matboard, or illustration board
Quick-drying glue
1" sponge brush
1" masking tape
Yardstick and measuring tape
Pencil, ruler, scissors, X-acto knife
  (optional)
1 dozen spring-loaded clothespins or
  large paper clips

Detail from color plate 9.

BANDBOXES were originally made to hold men's collar bands. It was soon recognized, however, that they were much more versatile, and they became widely used by both men and women for travel as well as storage. Their popularity reached a peak between the 1820s and 1850s. During this period, Americans were traveling about in record numbers, and bandboxes served as luggage to transport much of their finery. Made of pasteboard or thin wood, these boxes came in many shapes and sizes, but were most commonly round or oval. The edges were hand-sewn with heavy thread, and the insides were lined with newspaper. The outsides were covered with wallpaper, often hand-blocked in a rich array of colors and designs.

Bandboxes were made by box and wallpaper manufacturers as well as by cottage craftspeople. The most well-known box maker was a New Hampshire woman by the name of Hannah Davis (1784–1863). Her beautiful and sturdy boxes, crafted from wood, were a commodity much sought after by the young women who worked in the textile mills of nineteenth-century New England. Because they were so well made, many examples of her work still exist.

Today, bandboxes are collected not only for their historical value, but also for their use as practical decorating accents. Displayed on shelves and table-tops or stacked one on top of another, they add a splash of color to a room, while providing extra storage space. They make beautiful, reusable gift boxes, a package the recipient will cherish as much as the gift it contains. Unfortunately, because of their newfound popularity, bandboxes in any condition are becoming increasingly difficult to find and, as such, are very expensive. You don't have to pay collectors' prices to own a set of bandboxes, however. Just gather up the supplies I have listed and get started. You will probably find — like me — that you can't stop with just one.

MAKING A BANDBOX

The following instructions are for an oval bandbox made from pattern D. The finished size of this box will be approximately 6½" wide by 10" long by 7" deep. It is a good idea to practice by making this particular box because I have given the exact cutting measurements. Once you become familiar with the method of construction, you can make any size box by following the basic instructions and substituting your own measurements. Remember, though, always to make the lid piece at least ⅛" larger on all sides than the bottom piece. Masking tape is used in place of a needle and thread to join the lid to the rim and the bottom to the side panel (1" masking tape is used for all but the very small boxes).

Patterns also are included for three smaller oval boxes (patterns A, B, and C) and a heart-shaped box (see the special instructions with the pattern on page 28). Patterns for round boxes of any size can be made with a compass. If you don't have a piece of cardboard big enough for the circumference of the box you want to make, make the side and rim pieces from two pieces of cardboard; overlap the ends at least 1" to strengthen the seam line and tape them together on both sides of the cardboard.

When choosing cardboard for the box, look for a medium-weight, pliable type. For the smaller boxes, you may be able to find enough around your home. For larger boxes, use either illustration board, show card, or matboard, available in art supply stores. Before placing your pattern pieces on any of these materials, notice that the cardboard rolls more easily in one direction than the other; always cut the side panel and lid rim to take advantage of this natural curl. Corrugated cardboard (the type used for packing boxes) can be used for the top and bottom pieces (its strength and resistance to warping make it especially suited for this purpose on large boxes), but don't try to use it for the side panel or rim because it's not flexible enough and will crimp and fold on the curves.

When choosing wallpaper for your bandbox, avoid heavy-weight vinyl or flocked papers. Some of the attractive stencil-like paper and wallpaper borders available today make excellent choices and can mimic the look of authentic hand-blocked paper.

CUTTING THE CARDBOARD, LINING, AND WALLPAPER

1. Transfer the pattern to the cardboard. Cut one bottom piece and label it "bottom." Using this as a pattern, trace around it to make a second piece for the top. *Before cutting,* measure and mark ⅛" from your pencil line all around the oval, then connect the marks to make an oval that is ⅛" larger than the bottom all the way around. (When you are making a round box, you can do this with a compass.) Cut out this piece for the top and label it "top."

2. Determine the circumference of the box (and the length of the side panel) by wrapping a measuring tape around the edge of the bottom piece. (See Figure 2-1.) To this measurement, add 1" for overlap to strengthen the seam. The circumference of pattern D is 26" plus 1" for overlap, or 27". Mark and cut the cardboard 27" long by 7" wide for the side panel. (I used 7" for the depth of this box, but you can make it whatever depth you wish by cutting the cardboard to that width.)

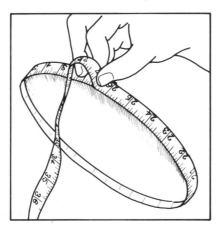

FIG. 2-1. *Determining the circumference of a box bottom.*

3. Determine the circumference of the lid (and the length of the lid rim piece) by wrapping a measuring tape around the edge of the lid; add 1" to this measurement for overlap. Mark and cut the cardboard 27½" long by 1" wide for pattern D. Unless you're making a very large or small box, a 1" width for the rim is standard.

4. Using the top, side, and bottom cardboard pieces as patterns, cut the lining pieces from newspaper to the exact size of the patterns (an X-acto knife works well for this cutting). The rim of the lid will be lined with wallpaper rather than newspaper.

5. Wallpaper will be used to cover the outside of the entire box, as well as the inside of the lid rim. The patterns can be traced on either side of the paper, although if you're trying to use only certain design elements of a wallpaper pattern, it's easier to trace on the right side; just remember to remove all pencil lines when the box is complete. Again using the cardboard pieces as patterns, cut the wallpaper as follows:

Lid: Cut a piece of wallpaper ½" larger all around than the cardboard lid piece. For ease in turning and a smoother fit when attaching it to the rim, make a series of V-shaped notches around the edge about ½" apart and *no deeper than* ⅜" (Figure 2-2).

(Text continues on page 26.)

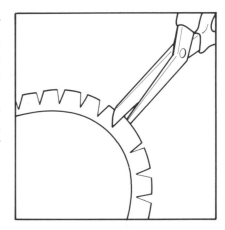

FIG. 2-2. *Cut V-notches around the edge of the wallpaper lid piece.*

Patterns for Bandbox Bottoms

NOTE: Remember always to cut the lid at least ⅛″ larger.

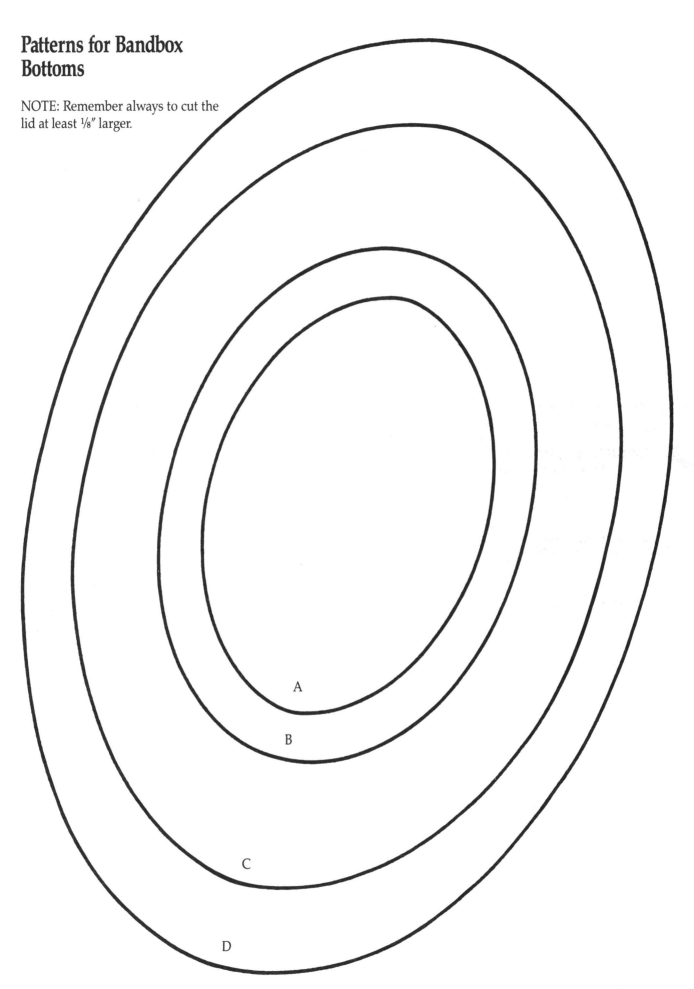

A

B

C

D

Lid rim: Cut a piece of wallpaper double the width of the rim plus ¼″, and the exact length of the rim piece: 2¼″ wide and 27½″ long for pattern D. To accent the rim, use a contrasting paper or a design element from the wallpaper (a row of flowers, for example).

Side panel: Trace around the side panel pattern, then measure and mark a ½″ overlap margin on each long side, making the wallpaper side piece 27″ long and 8″ wide for pattern D. (Use a smaller margin on very small bandboxes.) Make a series of V-shaped notches ½″ apart on one edge only.

Bottom: Cut a piece of wallpaper the same size as the pattern.

MAKING THE BOX BOTTOM

1. With the sponge brush, spread glue over one side of the side panel. Be sure to cover the cardboard completely, except for about ½″ at one end. (The glue will spread more easily if it is thinned slightly with water or applied with a moist brush.) Press the lining in place, leaving the unglued ½″ at one end unlined. This will mean you have an extra ½″ of lining at the other end — don't fold it over; it will be used to cover the inside seam. Allow the glue to dry. The paper may pucker slightly, but it should smooth out when the box is assembled.

2. Cut a strip of masking tape to the exact length of the side panel (27″ for pattern D). Stand the bottom piece on its edge in the center of the tape and wrap the tape completely around the edge of the bottom piece. (See Figure 2-3.) Press the tape

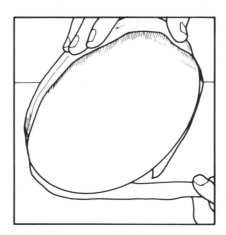

FIG. 2-3. *Wrap masking tape around the bottom edge.*

against the cardboard *on one side only,* while making sure the tape on the reverse side is as erect as possible. (See Figure 2-4.)

FIG. 2-4. *The tape should be erect on one side.*

3. Form the side panel into an oval shape, slightly smaller than the box bottom, with the unlined end covered by the end with the overlap. Place this oval inside the erect rim of tape on the bottom piece; position the middle of the side panel to meet the tape first. Then slowly and carefully expand the oval side panel to conform to the exact shape of the box bottom, pressing the tape to the edge of the side panel as you go. Check to be sure that the top edge of the side panel is perpendicular to the bottom; the sides should not slant inward or outward at any point. If they are positioned perfectly, you will have a 1″ overlap where the two ends of the side panel come together. (See Figure 2-5.) Press the tape firm-

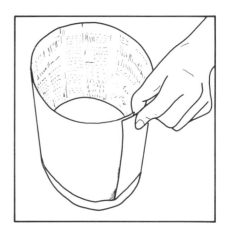

FIG. 2-5. *Positioning the side panel.*

ly along the bottom edge. Hold the side seam together at the top edge with a clothespin until it is secure. First, carefully spread glue on the inside of the ½″ liner overlap and press it flat to cover the seam. Then cut a strip of tape about 2″ longer than the width of the side panel (9″ for pattern D). Wrap about ¼″ of tape over the inside top edge, then run it down along the seam line (on the outside only), wrapping the excess onto the bottom of the box. Strengthen the seam by covering it with four to six more strips of tape and overlapping them onto the bottom and inside the top edge of the box. (See Figure 2-6.) The tape inside the top edge will be covered by the ½″ margin of wallpaper that will be folded over the edge when the wallpaper side piece is glued on in step 5.

4. Spread glue thoroughly on the inside of the box bottom and press the bottom lining in place.

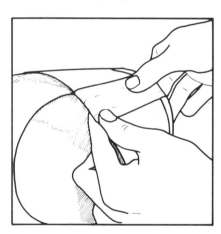

Fig. 2-6. *Taping the side panel.*

5. Spread glue on the wallpaper side piece, making sure its entire surface is covered. Lay the box on its side and centered on the wallpaper, with the notched edge of the wallpaper at the bottom edge of the box and a ½″ margin on both sides. Wrap the paper around the box, smoothing it as you go along. (See Figure 2-7.) Fold and press the unnotched top margin to the inside edge of the box and hold it in place with clothespins or paper clips until dry (Figure 2-8). Glue the notched margin to the bottom of the box, then cover the entire bottom with glue and press the bottom piece of wallpaper in place. When it is dry, trim the paper if necessary.

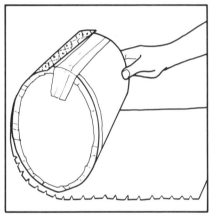

Fig. 2-7. *Wrapping the wallpaper around the side panel.*

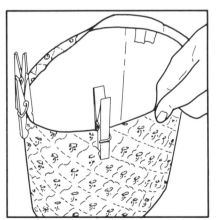

Fig. 2-8. *Hold the wallpaper in place with clothespins.*

MAKING THE LID

1. Attach the rim to the top piece, following steps 2 and 3 under Making the Box Bottom; adjust the length of the tape for the rim accordingly (27½″ for pattern D). Before continuing with the next step, check the fit of your lid by placing it on the box. Adjust it if necessary, but don't make it too tight; allow for the wallpaper that will be added to the lid in step 2.

2. Spread glue evenly on the outside of the lid and ½″ around the top edge of the rim, then smooth the wallpaper lid piece in place, folding the notched edge over the rim. Cover the outside of the rim with glue; position the rim paper on the glued area and smooth it in place. Spread glue on the inside of the rim, then fold the paper over and smooth it in place. Cover the inside of the lid with glue and press the lining in place. Hold the rim paper in place with clothespins until the glue is dry.

3. For an added decorative touch, glue a strip of thin velvet or grosgrain ribbon or lace around the rim, or glue a bow to the center of the lid.

MAKING A HEART-SHAPED BANDBOX

To make a heart-shaped bandbox, follow all the basic instructions except for the cutting of the rim and side pieces. To make these pieces, find half the circumference of the top and bottom heart pieces. Using this measurement for the length, cut two strips of cardboard each for the side panel and the lid rim. Butt the two side panel strips together and join them with masking tape, making a hinge. Repeat for the two lid rim strips. You will not be overlapping the cardboard at any time on the heart-shaped box. The taped hinge will form the bottom point of the heart. Finish the box according to the basic instructions.

Pattern for Bottom of Heart-Shaped Bandbox

NOTE: Remember to cut the lid at least ⅛" larger.

Scherenschnitte: Paper Cutting

*S*CHERENSCHNITTE (pronounced sharon-shnit-ta), German for "scissors cutting," was widely practiced in America by the German settlers of Pennsylvania during the eighteenth and nineteenth centuries. They used this technique to create beautiful, lace-like paper embellishments for marriage and birth certificates, as well as for love letters and house blessings. Love, friendship, and happiness were common themes in their paper cuttings, and these sentiments were symbolized by the use of certain motifs, the most common of which were hearts and hands, birds, tulips, and angels. Children as well as adults enjoyed this craft, and their deftly cut creations were often hung proudly on the family Christmas tree.

With the advent of the Industrial Revolution, the tradition of paper cutting began to wane. Many of the items once made by hand — valentines, paper dolls, marriage and birth certificates, Christmas decorations — could now be mass-produced and sold at such a reasonable cost that those who continued to make them by hand were often looked down upon and considered time wasters. As a result, the once cherished tradition of paper cutting was gradually forgotten, a casualty of progress.

But in this age of robotics and personal computers, interest in paper cutting is enjoying a renaissance. Perhaps this is due in part to the diametric simplicity of paper cutting. For literally pennies and a small investment in time, you can create wonderfully romantic one-of-a-kind gifts and unique framed pieces for your home. And paper cutting is such a relaxing craft, a welcome repose in an often too hectic world. Whatever the reason, why not give it a try? You might find that paper cutting is not just for kids!

SUPPLIES
Tracing and graphite paper
Calligrapher's parchment paper or typing paper
Transparent tape or stapler
Pencil
Small, sharp scissors such as Iris surgical scissors, embroidery scissors, or straight-tipped manicure scissors
Glue stick or spray adhesive and matboard for mounting
X-acto knife and pane of glass for cutting surface (optional)

MAKING SCHERENSCHNITTE

1. Trace the pattern onto the tracing paper.

2. Fold a sheet of parchment or typing paper in half and place the traced pattern on top of the paper; the dotted fold line of the pattern should be on the fold of the paper. Slip a sheet of graphite paper between these two and trace the design. Before removing the pattern, check to be sure all lines were transferred.

3. Staple or tape together the three open sides of the parchment paper.

4. Starting near the folded edge of the design, cut away the small areas first. By starting at the center of the design and cutting outward, you will have a larger area of paper to hold while working. When cutting out the small areas, begin by pushing the points of the scissors through the center of the design area (Figure 2-9). Then use the hole to start the cut.

FIG. 2-9. *Begin by making a hole with the point of the scissors.*

Detail from color plate 1.

Keep a constant pressure on the scissors and cut out each area with one continuous line whenever possible. Use your other hand to turn the paper in the direction of the cut. This will help ensure a smoother edge. If you find it difficult to use scissors, try an X-acto knife (Figure 2-10) — but make sure the surface beneath is protected with a pane of glass. You can pierce small holes with a needle, larger ones with a hole punch.

FIG. 2-10. *Cutting along the lines with an X-acto knife.*

5. Carefully remove the tape or staples and unfold the design. The side on which you traced the pattern will be the back. Place the design between two pieces of clean, white paper and press with a warm, dry iron to remove the crease.

OPTIONAL FINISHING TECHNIQUES

1. To simulate the foxing (yellowish brown stains) so common on many antique prints and papers, antique your finished cutting (parchment-paper cuttings only) by staining it with a tea solution. Begin by soaking a tea bag in a small amount of hot water until the solution is quite strong. Squeeze most of the excess moisture from the bag, then dab the bag on the surface of your paper cutting, gently squeezing as you go to release enough tea to achieve a mottled look. It's a good idea to practice this on a piece of scrap paper before going to your cutting. For additional antiquing, dip an old toothbrush in the solution and lightly spatter the cutting (see Chapter 1–Antiquing, page 21).

2. If you prefer the look of a dark cutting matted on a light background, spray your finished design with several light coats of flat black paint.

3. The beauty of many scherenschnitte patterns can be enhanced and given a fraktur-like quality if you paint the design with watercolors or thinned stencil paint. (Frakturs were another method by which the early German settlers recorded important events. The design motifs on these certificates, similar to those used on paper cuttings, were hand-painted, and the dates were recorded in elaborate script.) For an authentic look, paint the design in subdued tones of red, blue, gold, brown, and green. Mix just enough water with your paint to make it flow freely and use a sable or taklon round brush. After the paint dries, you can add more color if you want a brighter look. Remember, you can't remove the paint if it is too dark, so build the color intensity gradually.

4. If you plan to frame your project, cut a piece of matboard to the size of your frame. Dab a small amount of glue on the back of the cutting or use a spray adhesive. Center the cutting on the matboard and press it in place. A nice effect can be achieved by mounting your design on small-patterned wallpaper.

(Text continues on page 36.)

Patterns for Scherenschnitte Angel and Heart Design

This design would make a wonderful birth or marriage certificate. You can personalize it with script-writing or calligraphy. It will also lend itself beautifully to the painting style described in step 3 under "Optional Finishing Techniques," page 30. Trace the pattern onto an 8" x 10" piece of parchment paper folded in half, and cut.

Edge of paper

Place on fold of paper.

Script Samples for Angel and Heart Design

____

and

____

were united in marriage

by ______________________________

the _______________ *day of* _____________,

the year ______________.

A child is born

____

Child's name

____

Date of birth

____

Place of birth

House with Willows Design

When framed, this design makes a truly delightful housewarming gift. I found it easier to cut this pattern with an X-acto knife than with scissors. When it is completed, you can personalize it with one of the following sayings:

Home is best

Bless this home

Welcome

Welcome friends

Home is where the heart is

The road to a friend's house is never long

Position the pattern on a 7″ x 9″ piece of parchment paper folded in half, and cut.

Detail from color plate 4.

Edge of paper

Place on fold of paper.

Noah's Ark Design

NOTE: Cut out clouds separately, as many as you want, and attach them to the matboard with a small dab of glue or spray adhesive.

Place on fold of paper.

Detail from color plate 2.

Birds in the Nest Design

Detail from color plate 9.

Place on fold of paper.

Love Birds Design

Detail from color plate 10.

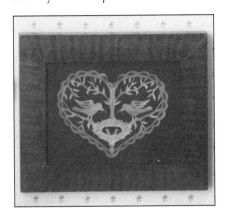

Place on fold of paper.

Tabletop Tree Ornament

Place on fold of paper.

TABLETOP TREE ORNAMENT

This festive design can be used to create a free-standing three-dimensional tabletop decoration, a delicate tree ornament, or a beautiful framed picture. Since this pattern is so angular, I found it easier to cut with an X-acto knife.

To make a tabletop tree, cut two trees from a medium-weight paper (construction paper works well). Place the folded tree on a terry towel and pierce through each dot with a large pin. Unfold both trees and place them together, matching the fold lines. Sew by hand (or with a sewing machine) along the fold. Spread the trees open to stand the ornament.

To make a tree ornament, take the pattern to a copier and reduce it to about one third its original size; transfer the pattern to typing or calligrapher's paper and follow the instructions in the preceding paragraph. Since you will be working on such a small scale, you may want to delete some of the details, the ornaments and candles. When you sew the trees together, leave about 4" of thread at the top for a hanger.

To make a seasonal wallhanging, cut a single tree out of parchment paper (reduce the pattern if desired), mount it on red or dark green velour paper, and frame it.

Detail from color plate 6.

Cut and Pierced Lampshades

THE beautiful lampshades in this section are made by using a combination of two very old techniques: paper cutting, or scherenschnitte (described in the previous section), and paper pinpricking.

Pinpricking has been practiced for centuries, but as a craft it reached a pinnacle of popularity in the early nineteenth century. At that time, the technique was used in many different and creative ways, some simple, and others more elaborate. One such example is *repoussé*, a method used to create pictures by pinpricking a design in paper and then elevating selected areas of the design by wetting the inside of the paper with water. After wetting, the area was stretched and shaped, sometimes with the back of a spoon, to get a rounded look. When the raised area was thoroughly dried, the inside of the paper was sized with thinned glue to ensure that the embossed area would hold its shape. The design was often painted, then mounted on black or gold-painted paper and framed. Although popular in its time, pinpricking was a relatively short-lived craft, and by the late nineteenth century, with the invention of the mechanical embossing machine, it had virtually disappeared.

Today, variations of cutting and pinpricking are combined in the making of cut and pierced lampshades. These unique shades can be made in a number of ways. The design can simply be cut and pierced; it can be stenciled or painted on the outside of the shade before cutting and piercing; or, for a really striking effect, a design can be stenciled or hand-painted on the inside of the shade so that it will glow with color when the lamp is lit. Each of these methods will be explained thoroughly. To become familiar with the required tools and techniques, read the general instructions before choosing a project.

Detail from color plate 10.

SUPPLIES

See each project for a complete list of supplies. The following paragraphs describe some of the less common items.

Shade paper: Lampshade paper is available in a rainbow of colors, making it possible to create a shade to match any color scheme. If you plan to paint or stencil a design on your shade, choose a light-colored paper (white, ivory, or a pastel). If you can't find lampshade paper, substitute a good quality medium-weight watercolor paper.

Lining paper: Lining paper, available in soft hues to match your shade paper, can usually be found in craft stores that carry lamp-making supplies. (See the Source Guide, page 159.) Medium- to heavy-weight tracing paper can be substituted.

Piercing and cutting tools: For piercing, use a lampshade piercing tool (it looks like a dowel with a needle embedded in each end). This tool can be found at most larger craft stores. If unavailable, use a large needle (for example, a yarn darner or a tapestry needle) or a corsage or hat pin. For an interesting effect, try piercing a design with different-size needles. For cutting the design, use an X-acto knife with a new No. 11 blade. To protect your work surface, do your cutting on a pane of window glass (tape the edges of the glass to prevent cuts).

Lampshade rings: You need a top and bottom ring for each lampshade. The exact size needed for each shade is given in the supply list preceding each project. Top rings are available in several styles: clip-on rings that clamp to the bulb, washer-top rings that screw onto harps, and chimney rings that fit over oil lamp chimneys. The type of lamp base you plan to use with your shade dictates this choice.

MAKING A LAMPSHADE

Because the pages of this book are not large enough to accommodate full-size lampshade patterns, a half pattern is given for the Heart, Pineapple, and Stenciled Kitten shades (pattern A, page 39); and one quarter of the full-size pattern is given for the Summer's Bounty shade, pattern B (page 40).

1. To make a full-size pattern from pattern A, you must first decide whether you want a scalloped or straight-edged shade (the straight-edged shade is trimmed with ribbon to finish the edges). You might even decide to use a straight edge on the top and a scalloped edge on the bottom. Trace the half pattern onto a folded piece of medium-weight tracing paper (folded size: 9″ x 10″). Be certain to transfer the center mark, as this will be used as a guide for centering the design in step 2. Hold the layers together so they won't shift and cut out the pattern. (Cut along the broken lines for a straight edge.) Unfold the paper and place the full-size pattern on the shade paper, secure it with small pieces of tape, and carefully trace around the pattern with a pencil. Transfer the center mark with a light pencil dot, then cut out the shade with an X-acto knife or scissors.

NOTE: You can make your own shade pattern by taking apart an old lampshade and tracing the shape onto shade paper.

2. Transfer the design (except for the stenciled shade) onto the tracing-paper pattern made in step 1. Center the design on the center mark of your shade, slip a piece of graphite paper between the layers, hold it in place (use tape if necessary), and trace lightly, transferring every dot and line as indicated on the pattern. This will be the inside of the shade. Do not connect any broken lines when tracing.

3. All painting or stenciling is done prior to cutting and piercing. See individual project instructions.

4. All areas to be pierced are marked on the pattern with a dot. Piercing is always done before cutting to prevent tearing the paper. Pierce on the side of the paper to which you have transferred the design. To begin, place your shade on a folded terry towel and, holding your piercing tool in an upright position, punch through the dots. Do not pierce closer than ⅛″ apart. (See Figure 2-11.)

FIG. 2-11. *Use a lampshade piercing tool for the dots.*

5. All areas to be cut are marked on the pattern with a solid dark line. Always cut on the side of the shade to which you transferred the design. Place the shade on a pane of glass and, using a sharp X-acto knife held like a pencil, cut along the solid lines. (See Figure 2-12.) Try to cut each line in one continuous stroke, always being conscious of where the line ends. When you reach a corner or a point (the tip of a leaf, for example), stop and, without lifting your knife, turn the paper and complete the cut. Leave at least ⅛″ of paper uncut between designs; you don't want to remove any whole pieces from the shade. For curves, move the paper rather than the knife as you cut.

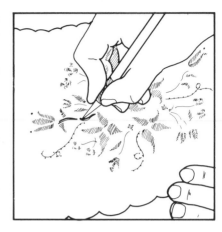

FIG. 2-12. *Cutting the design with an X-acto knife.*

6. Sculpting adds dimension to the design and allows additional light to shine through. Using the handle of your piercing tool, the side of a pencil, or your fingers, gently curl chosen sections of the design (leaves and petals, for example) toward the inside of the shade. (See Figure 2-13.) To be certain that you haven't missed a section, periodically hold the paper up to a light as you work. Highlight the straight-cut areas that can't be curled (stems, for example) by inserting a needle or the end of the piercer into the cut, then using a back-and-forth motion to open it up slightly.

(Text continues on page 41.)

FIG. 2-13. *Sculpting the cut design.*

Lampshade Pattern A

1. Cut along broken line for a
   straight-edged shade.
2. Broken line indicates placement
   line for the rings.

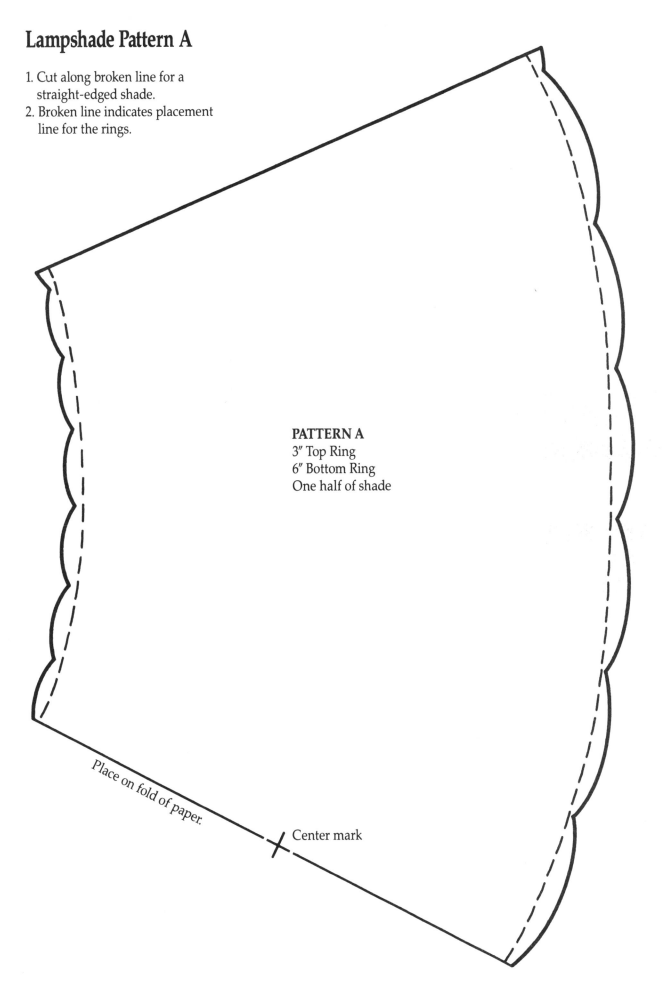

PATTERN A
3″ Top Ring
6″ Bottom Ring
One half of shade

Place on fold of paper.

Center mark

Lampshade Pattern B

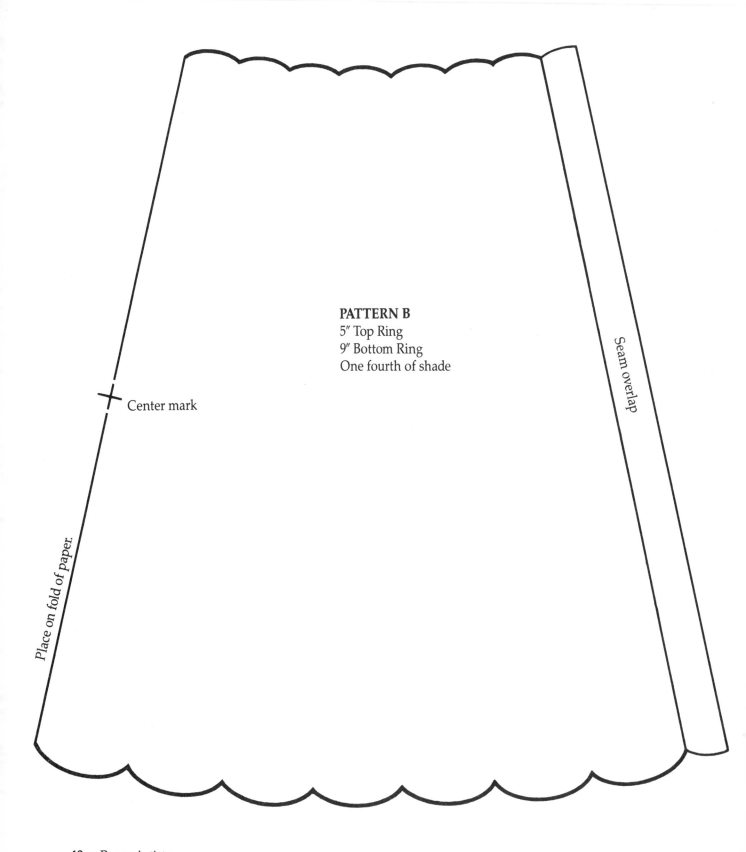

PATTERN B
5″ Top Ring
9″ Bottom Ring
One fourth of shade

Center mark

Place on fold of paper.

Seam overlap

7. I prefer to line my shades for two reasons: Lining prevents the bulb from showing through the sculpted areas, thereby giving the shade a more finished appearance, and it also diffuses the light, making a prettier glow. Line your shade only after all painting, piercing, and sculpting have been completed. Using the shade as a pattern, cut the lining paper ½" larger all around than the shade. With a small brush, spread a thin line of glue along the inside of the upper edge and both ends of the shade (keep it as close to the edge as possible); press the lining in place. Then spread glue along the bottom edge of the shade and press the bottom of the lining in place, easing in fullness around the sculpted areas of the design. Don't try to get the lining to fit smoothly; it should look somewhat wrinkled and puffy. This puffiness prevents the sculpted areas from being flattened when the shade is attached to the rings. Turn the shade over, lining side down, and with an X-acto knife, carefully trim the excess lining paper so that it is even with the edge of the shade.

8. Because straight-edged shades are trimmed with ribbon, it is important that the rings be attached flush with the top and bottom edges. On a scalloped shade, attach the rings even with the inner edges of the scallop trim (the broken lines on pattern A). Have a damp cloth handy to remove any traces of misplaced glue before they dry.

Bottom ring: Run a bead of glue along the inside bottom edge of the shade. Working quickly (the glue dries fast) and holding the ring like a wheel, start at one end and roll the ring into the line of glue, wrapping the edge up and around the ring as you go (Figure 2-14). Secure with

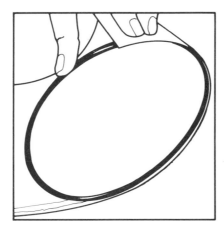

FIG. 2-14. *Wrapping the shade around the ring.*

clothespins every 2" or so. (See Figure 2-15.) Use a clothespin to hold the side seam together while the bottom dries. To avoid leaving a mark on your shade, grip the rings with the flat area of the clothespin. (See Figure 2-15b.) Remove the clothespins when the glue is dry.

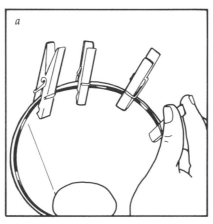

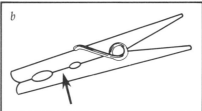

FIG. 2-15. *Hold the bottom ring in place (a), using the flat part of the clothespin to grip (b).*

Top ring: Spread a thin line of glue along the inside top edge of the shade, then turn the shade upside down and lower the ring into position. (See Figure 2-16.) Adjust the paper to fit, turn the shade right side up, and hold the ring in place with clothespins until the glue is dry.

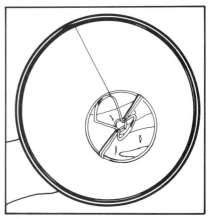

FIG. 2-16. *Dropping the top ring into the shade.*

Side seam: With a small brush, spread glue under the seam overlap. With one hand on the outside and one on the inside, press and hold the seam flat until the glue is dry — two to three minutes. Check to be sure there are no areas where a ring has pulled away from the shade. Reglue if necessary. On a straight-edged shade, trim any shade paper that extends above or below the rings. (See Figure 2-17.)

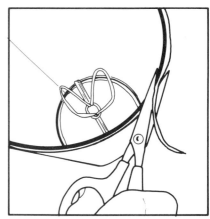

FIG. 2-17. *Trim the paper edges with scissors.*

9. For a finished look on straight-edged shades, trim the edge of the shade with ⅝″ (No. 3) grosgrain ribbon in a matching or contrasting color. (It's difficult to get glue to stick to 100 percent polyester, so try to use ribbon made from a cotton-rayon blend.) To determine how much ribbon you will need, measure the circumference of the top and bottom rings and add 1″ for overlap for each piece.

One third of the ribbon width will be on the front of the shade; the remaining two thirds will be wrapped to the inside. Using your fingers or an iron, press a fold in the ribbon accordingly. (See Figure 2-18.) Attach one half at a time. Starting at the seam (top of the shade), apply glue to the outside edge of the shade and stick the ribbon in place, pulling it to keep it taut and wrinkle-free. Complete the other half, then overlap and glue the ends. Snip the ribbon where

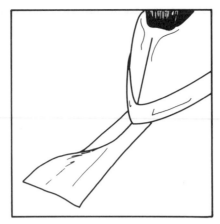

FIG. 2-18. *Press a fold in the ribbon.*

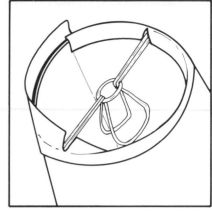

FIG. 2-19. *Snip the ribbon around the spokes.*

the spokes on the top ring are located so it will fit smoothly around them (Figure 2-19). Spread glue on the inside edge of the ribbon and roll it to the inside of the shade to cover the ring. Press it firmly around the ring. Turn the shade upside down and glue ribbon to the bottom edge in the same way.

For an added decorative touch, double-trim the shade edge with thin (⅛″ to ¼″) velvet or satin ribbon in a contrasting color. Spread glue on the ribbon and place it about ¼″ from the edge of the shade, slightly overlapping the grosgrain ribbon. Butt the ends at the back of the shade.

Cut and Pierced Heart or Pineapple Shade

SUPPLIES
9″ x 20″ sheet of tracing paper
Pencil
12″ x 15″ sheet of lampshade paper
Transparent tape
X-acto knife and pane of glass
Scissors
Graphite paper
Piercer and towel
12″ x 15″ sheet of lining paper
Small bristle brush
Tacky glue
Lampshade rings (3″ top, 6″ bottom)
Clothespins

BECAUSE these charming, diminutive shades require no painting or stenciling, they're the perfect project for a beginner. When finished, use them wherever soft, subdued atmosphere lighting is desired. Since the pineapple is a symbol of hospitality, place this shade in a hall or foyer to extend a warm, glowing welcome on a cold winter's night.

MAKING THE SHADE

Follow the instructions given under Making a Lampshade (page 38) and use pattern A (page 39) to make either the Heart or Pineapple shade. The Heart design is on page 43, the Pineapple on page 44.

Detail from color plate 9.

Cut and Pierced Heart Design

Use with Lampshade Pattern A. Cut on solid lines; pierce on dots. Plus sign (+) is the center of the heart — do *not* pierce.

NOTE: Use edge design on scalloped shade only.

Cut and Pierced Pineapple Design

Use with Lampshade Pattern A.
Cut on solid lines; pierce on dots.
Plus sign (+) is the center of the
pineapple — do *not* pierce.

NOTE: Use edge design on
scalloped shade only.

Stenciled Kitten Shade

I T SEEMS we all know someone who just loves cats, and wouldn't this shade add the finishing touch to a collection of cat paraphernalia? The design is stenciled on the outside of the shade before cutting or piercing. (If you are unfamiliar with stencil cutting and stenciling, refer to Chapter 4 before beginning.) If you don't know a single cat fancier, choose another stencil of comparable size and omit step 2. When using your own stencil, carefully study the design to decide which parts will be pierced and which will be cut. It might help to make a piercing and cutting diagram for your stencil before beginning. Then complete the shade according to the general instructions.

SUPPLIES
9″ x 20″ sheet of tracing paper
Pencil
12″ x 15″ sheet of lampshade paper (white or pastel)
Transparent tape
X-acto knife and pane of glass
Scissors
5″ x 5″ sheet of Mylar
Acrylic paint (Folk Art colors: Dove Gray, Cherokee Rose, Clover Green, black)
Two stencil brushes
No. 1 round brush
Piercer and towel
12″ x 15″ sheet of lining paper
Small bristle brush
Tacky glue
Lampshade rings (3″ top, 6″ bottom)
Clothespins

MAKING THE SHADE

1. Cut out pattern A (page 39) following step 1 under Making a Lampshade (page 38).

2. Place a sheet of Mylar (frosted side up) over the stencil design below; then trace the design outline and center mark. Place the Mylar on a pane of glass and cut out the Mylar stencil with an X-acto knife.

3. Center the stencil on one half of the shade, tape it in place (remove some of the tape's stickiness beforehand by pressing it on a piece of fabric), and stencil using Dove Gray for the kittens and Cherokee Rose for the ball of yarn and bows.

Remove the stencil and clean off any traces of paint. Turn the stencil over and reposition it on the other half of the shade by aligning the stencil center mark with the center mark on the shade. Make sure the stencil is the same distance from the bottom edge on both halves of the shade (the bottom of the kitten's tail should be about 1½″ from the edge of the shade). Stencil to complete the design, stenciling the ball of yarn only once. Using a No. 1 round brush, paint the eyes Clover Green with small black pupils.

(Text continues on next page.)

Detail from color plate 2.

Kitten Shade Stencil Pattern

NOTE: This is a half pattern; turn over to complete the design.

Center mark
+

4. See steps 4 and 5 under Making a Lampshade, page 38. Place the shade on a folded towel and pierce the pupils and a series of evenly spaced dots (four to a group) all over the shade. Use Figure 2-20 as a guide. Then, working from the outside of the shade and referring to Figure 2-20, cut where indicated by the solid lines, remembering to leave at least ⅛" of paper between cuts. *Do not cut out the whole kitten.*

5. To complete the shade, refer to steps 6-9 under Making a Lampshade, pages 38–42.

FIG. 2-20. *Cutting guide for the kitten lampshade.*

Center mark

NOTE: *Do not transfer to the shade. Use only as a guide for cutting and piercing the shade.*

Summer's Bounty Painted Shade

A FLORAL design is painted on the inside of this shade so that when the light is out, the shade has the look of a lovely piece of candlewicking. But its real beauty can be appreciated only when the lamp is lit; then every detail of its delicately painted design is illuminated, creating a truly sensational, one-of-a-kind lampshade.

SUPPLIES

Two 16″ x 10″ sheets of tracing paper
Pencil
Paper clips
Scissors
Transparent tape
Lampshade rings (5″ top, 9″ bottom)
Clothespins
Graphite paper
18″ x 24″ sheet of lampshade paper (white)
Acrylic paint (Folk Art colors: Cherokee Rose, Patchwork Green, Clover, Bluebell, Buttercup, Honey Comb) Note: You may use watercolors if you prefer.
No. 2 and No. 4 round (sable or taklon) brushes
Piercer and towel
X-acto knife and pane of glass
18″ x 24″ sheet of lining paper
Small bristle brush
Tacky glue

Detail from color plate 4.

MAKING THE SHADE

1. Fold both sheets of tracing paper in half, making two 8″ x 10″ pieces. Place the folded edge of one sheet along the fold line on pattern B (page 40) and trace all lines. Slip the blank sheet of tracing paper inside the other, folds together and all edges even. Secure the layers at the fold line with paper clips. Cut carefully along the pattern outline, being careful not to shift the layers. The seam overlap is needed on only one end, so remove the excess paper by cutting along the seam overlap line on the top three layers. Remove the clips and unfold the two sheets of paper. Shift the top layer of the pattern to the left, butt the pattern halves together (seam overlap on the right), and tape.

2. Trace the full-size pattern onto shade paper and cut it out.

3. Transfer the design (page 48) to the center of the inside of the shade according to the instructions in step 2 under Making a Lampshade, page 38.

4. Mix a little water with your paint to achieve a smooth-flowing, nearly transparent mixture. Since the intensity of the color is dependent on the amount of water added to the paint, practice your painting on a scrap of shade paper before painting on the shade, then hold the sample up to a bare bulb. If it is too light, add less water to your paint. Shading or highlighting is not necessary, as sculpting (step 6, page 38) will add another dimension to the design. With the round brushes, paint the inside of the shade as follows: roses and buds Cherokee Rose, some leaves Patchwork Green and some Clover, small flowers and tulips Bluebell with Buttercup centers, some tendrils Honey Comb and some Clover, and the tiny dotted clusters Buttercup.

5. Pierce and cut the shade as explained under Making a Lampshade, steps 4 and 5 (page 38). If the cutting lines are not visible through the paint, refer to the pattern.

6. Sculpt the design, line the shade, and attach the shade to the rings as explained in steps 6–9 (pages 38–42).

Summer's Bounty Painted Shade

Use with Lampshade Pattern B.
Cut on solid lines; pierce on dots.
Plus sign (+) is the center of the
design — do *not* pierce.

3
Kitchen and Garden Crafts

THE KITCHEN is often referred to as "the heart of the home," and with good reason, for it is here that so many hours are spent preparing and sharing meals in the company of family and friends. In this chapter, you will discover that many things gathered from the garden and from your kitchen shelf can be fashioned into charming decorative items for every room in your home. Included are many ideas for capturing the essence of the seasons and bringing them into your home to enjoy all year long. You will discover that the pleasure is not only in the making of these projects, but also in the gathering of the materials.

Decorating with natural materials can add a warm, welcoming, country feeling to any room in your home. Kitchens, no matter how modern and efficient, become cozy and inviting when filled with the scent of a fragrant wreath or a simmering potpourri. Antique wooden or glass bowls filled to the brim with a favorite potpourri and placed strategically throughout your home will look as beautiful as they smell. Or welcome your guests and herald the changing seasons with a pretty front door decoration or wreath. Even in your bathroom, a natural sachet can make a soothing bath much more luxurious. All these ideas and more can be found in this chapter.

Scratched-Carved Eggs

SUPPLIES

1 dozen large white eggs (uncooked)
2 cups of tightly packed red or yellow onion skins (dry outer skins only)
A few drops of vinegar
2 quarts of water
Large glass, enamel, or stainless-steel pot
Tracing and graphite paper, or white chalk sewing pencil
Terry towel (optional)
Large pin, X-acto knife, or single-edged razor blade
Spray acrylic sealer

Detail from color plate 6.

I REMEMBER, as a small child, walking into my grandmother's kitchen the week before Easter and, much to my surprise and dismay, finding her coloring her eggs brown and with, of all things, onion skins! I mused over why, with a kaleidoscope of colors available, she would resort to such an unusual practice. It wasn't until many years later that I came to understand the tradition and appreciate the unusual beauty of the craft she lovingly passed on to me.

Long before the refinement of commercial dyes, our inventive ancestors used berries, barks, flowers, roots, and, yes, even onion skins as dyes. The custom of scratch-carving Easter eggs originated with the Pennsylvania Dutch. Unlike many egg crafts, in which the contents of the eggs are removed and discarded, scratched-carved eggs are left full to preserve their significance as a symbol of life. It takes from six months to a year for the contents of the eggs to dry out. When completely dry, the yolk will shrivel and make a rattling sound inside the shell when shaken.

The eggs are first boiled in water with onion skins, thus being cooked and dyed simultaneously. Then designs are made on the egg by scratching away the dye with a pointed tool to reveal the white shell underneath. When this is done on a very dark shell, the finished egg often resembles scratch-decorated redware pottery (*sgraffito*). Designs using classic Pennsylvania Dutch motifs such as hearts, tulips, and birds were commonly used (see the patterns on page 51), but you can experiment and let their inspiration lead you to your own creations. Try integrating animals or birds into your patterns; the scratching technique is perfect for doing fur or feathers. Or start a holiday tradition by personalizing eggs with names and dates and presenting them to family and friends on Easter Sunday. If handled and stored carefully, these eggs can be displayed and cherished for years.

MAKING SCRATCHED-CARVED EGGS

1. Remove the eggs from the refrigerator and bring them to room temperature. This will reduce the risk of cracking from the temperature change while cooking. Some egg processors coat their eggs with an oily or waxy film to retard spoilage. Because this film might affect the dying process, resulting in blotchy colors, always wash eggs thoroughly before dying.

2. Place the eggs, onion skins, vinegar, and water in a pot. Be certain that the tops of the eggs are completely covered and the sides are not touching. Slowly bring the water to a boil, reduce the heat to a simmer, and cook for thirty minutes to one hour. The intensity of the color is determined by how long the eggs simmer in the dye. Simmer a short time for a light brown; a longer simmering time will produce a rich burgundy. Turn the eggs while cooking so they will dye evenly. When they have reached a desirable shade, remove them from the water with a slotted spoon and drain them in an egg carton or on paper towels. If you plan to color eggs again, strain the onion broth through a sieve to remove the skins. The dye may be kept in a covered container in the refrigerator for several days.

3. The designs in this chapter can be traced (just the outline) and then transferred to the egg with graphite paper, or try sketching your own simple design onto the eggs with a chalk pencil. Cradle the egg gently in the palm of your hand while scratch-

carving, or rest it on a folded terry towel (Figure 3-1). Work slowly and carefully, as mistakes are difficult to correct. Begin by etching in the outline of your design with the point of your blade or needle. Then study your design and decide where the light and the dark areas will be.

To highlight an area, remove the dye with a series of side-by-side scratch lines. The deeper you scratch the shell, the whiter your design will become, but be careful not to cut through the shell. Crosshatching (Figure 3-2) can be used to give texture to the design, or you can remove whole areas of dye by scratching the shell with the edge of a razor blade. But remember, don't apply too much pressure on the egg, or it might break. If the shell cracks — even a hairline crack — the egg must be discarded. To shade (inside the rabbit's ear, for example), leave the dye intact.

4. When your design is complete, spray the egg with several light coats of acrylic sealer to strengthen and protect the shell. When they are not on display, store the eggs inside an egg carton in a dry room (an attic works well).

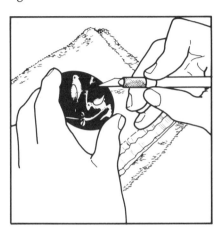

FIG. 3-1. *Rest the egg on a folded terry towel while carving.*

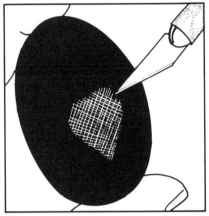

FIG. 3-2. *Crosshatching gives texture to a design.*

Patterns for Scratched-Carved Eggs

Drying Flowers and Herbs

FLOWERS FOR FRAGRANCE
Chamomile
Honeysuckle
Lavender
Marigolds
Pinks
Roses

FRAGRANT HERBS
Bay leaf
Lemon balm
Lemon verbena
Marjoram
Mint
Rosemary
Sage
Scented geranium leaves
Sweet woodruff
Thyme

MID-MORNING on a dry sunny day is the best time to harvest flowers, herbs, and leaves for drying. Since dampness will impede the drying process and affect color retention, wait until all the morning dew has evaporated. (For me, morning is the most pleasant time for being in the garden, and a beautiful, relaxing way to start the day.) Pick flowers just before they reach their peak of development — petals should not be faded. Choose herbs just as their buds are opening into full bloom; at this point the leaves contain the greatest amount of volatile oils, which results in the most fragrance. Gather only as much as you can dry in one day.

Some dried plants retain their fragrance and color much better than others. Many flowers intensify in color, others fade to a muted shade, while still others turn a disappointing brown. The list below is a sampling of some of the best flowers and herbs to use for making potpourri and wreaths. But be creative! Test-dry whatever you have on hand — you might be pleasantly surprised.

DRYING METHODS

Hang drying: Before hang-drying flowers (not herbs), strip the leaves from the stems. Wrap the ends of six to twelve stems (depending on the size) together with a small rubber band. (Since the stems shrink as they dry, a rubber band will hold them better than string.) Hang them upside-down in a warm, dry, airy but shady place. Exposure to sunlight will cause the colors to fade. Flowers and herbs should be dry in one to two weeks. Remove the herb leaves and the flower petals from their stems and store them whole in airtight containers until you are ready to use them.

Air drying: Strip flower petals and herb leaves from their stems and place them in a single layer between two window screens. The screens should be elevated at least 1' from the ground (on bricks, for example) and placed in a dry, airy spot, protected from the sun, weather, and dew. Inspect and stir the petals and leaves periodically; they should dry within a week. Store whole leaves and petals in airtight containers away from direct light. (The scent is best if they are left whole for storage, then crumbled as needed.)

POTPOURRI

A potpourri is a mixture of dried flowers, herbs, and spices blended together with a fixative (orrisroot being the most common) to preserve the fragrance and scented oils that intensify the bouquet. Rose petals and buds often make up the bulk of potpourri blends, but many other flowers and leaves can be used. (Refer to the lists on this page.)

Potpourri can be used in many ways. To scent stationery, make a small tissue-paper envelope, fill it with potpourri, and tuck it into the stationery box. Fill decorative containers with a favorite blend and place them around your home or office. Make an old-fashioned sachet by wrapping potpourri inside a pretty lace-trimmed handkerchief or piece of fabric; tie with a satin ribbon and tuck into drawers, closets, and blanket chests. Make cleaning day less of a chore by adding a choice potpourri to your vacuum cleaner bag (or simply saturate a cotton ball with an essential oil and tuck it into a new bag).

I always keep a large wooden bowl of potpourri on my dining table. It doesn't have a chance to get faded or stale because the ingredients are constantly changing. I rarely throw away a flower — not those from a birthday bouquet or corsage or the wildflowers picked by our little girl. Instead, while the flowers are still at their peak, I simply strip the petals from the stems and add them to the mixture (in some cases I place the whole flower in the bowl). Don't put too many in at once, though, and be sure to stir the blend periodically while a new addition is drying; the dry ingredients in the bowl will draw the remaining moisture from the petals. In this way, my potpourri is constantly growing. When it begins to overflow the bowl, I simply remove some to use as a base for a new blend. In an open bowl the scent dissipates more quickly than in a closed container, but that's a small price to pay for the constant visual and aromatic pleasures it provides.

Because each person's sense of smell is unique, this basic potpourri recipe can be altered to suit personal tastes. It will last forever, requiring only a little freshening with an essential oil when the scent begins to fade. (Essential oils can usually be found at craft stores, floral centers, or health food stores.)

BASIC RECIPE
1 tablespoon of orrisroot
8 drops of rose or lavender oil
1 quart of dried rose petals
½ cup each of rosebuds, rose geranium leaves, lemon verbena, lavender flowers, mint leaves, rosemary, and lemon balm
1 crushed cinnamon stick
5 ground cloves
1 teaspoon of cardamom

Mix the orrisroot with the oil. Combine all the dry ingredients in a large bowl and sprinkle with the orrisroot mixture. Blend all the ingredients and store in a large covered container in a cool, dark, dry place for one month. Stir gently once or twice a week.

BATH SACHETS
If you've never tried a bath sachet, set some time aside for an unforgettably enjoyable and relaxing experience. Store the dried leaves of mint, lemon balm, rose geranium, or any other fragrant flower or herb, and the dried petals from lavender, chamomile, marigolds (soothes exposed summer skin), or roses in pretty glass jars in your bathroom. Before drawing your bath, steep ½ cup of one or a combination of several in boiling water for about fifteen minutes. Strain into your bath water and enjoy. (Instead of steeping the loose leaves, you can wrap the blend in cheesecloth or place it inside a tea ball and drop it in the bath water.)

Or you can wrap the blend in muslin or a washcloth, tie it closed with a piece of twine, and hang it from the faucet in your tub. Upon entering your bath, swish the sachet around in the hot water to release its scent. Hang it from the faucet to dry afterwards; you can use it several more times before discarding the herbs.

Herb Wreath

SUPPLIES
Thin wire for hanging
10" to 12" straw wreath base
Florist's U pins and picks
Scissors
Hot-glue gun or tacky glue (optional)
Base materials: silver king artemisia
** or German statice**
5" sprigs of any of the following herbs:
** sage, rosemary, thyme, lamb's ear,**
** lavender, purple basil, tarragon**
Dried flower suggestions: oregano
** flowers, yarrow, strawflowers,**
** cockscomb, chive flowers, globe**
** amaranth, nigella pods**
Cinnamon sticks, bay leaves, whole
** nutmeg**

IF YOU are fortunate enough to have an herb garden, you know that summer is the time it is bursting with growth. To encourage continued new growth through the remaining months, treat your plants to a healthy cutting back — and what better use for all those cuttings than an herb wreath!

You can use fresh or dried herbs to fashion this beautiful, versatile wreath. I prefer to use fresh herbs because they are easier to work with and they dry beautifully right on the wreath. In the kitchen, enjoy the wreath simply for its fragrance, or snip the leaves as needed and add them to a favorite recipe. When it is not hanging, use it as an attractive centerpiece or decorative candle ring. Choose from among the herbs I have listed or create your own design with whatever you have on hand. Remember, the beauty of the wreath is not only in its scent, but also in the varied textures and contrasting colors of the herbs and flowers. If you don't have an herb garden, or are not lucky enough to have a friend or neighbor who does, you can order the herbs and flowers in the supply list from the companies listed in the Source Guide on page 159.) The finished size of this wreath will be 3" to 4" larger than the base.

MAKING AN HERB WREATH

1. Attach a wire loop to the back of the wreath base for hanging; then, using florist's pins, begin attaching large sprays of base material (see the supply list) along the sides of the base in a clockwise direction. Each spray should cover the stems of the preceding one, until the outside edge is completely covered. (Periodically, hang the wreath, stand back to look, and check it for symmetry.) When the outside edge is covered, break the artemisia or statice into smaller sprays and fill in the front and inside edge, completely covering the straw base. (See Decorated Straw Hat, page 56, for tips on working with statice.) Make it full, as this will serve as the foundation for the herbs and flowers.

2. Begin attaching herbs, choosing colors that contrast with those of the base materials. Once again working in a clockwise direction, pin the herbs to the outer edges first, then to the front and inside. Pin on additional herbs, then flowers, to add different textures and colors. Try to choose colors that will coordinate with the colors of the room in which you'll be using the wreath. Cinnamon sticks, nutmeg, and bay leaves can be attached with a hot-glue gun or tacky glue.

3. The herbs will eventually lose their fragrance, but you can refresh your wreath by using fresh herbs to replace those that have faded.

Detail from color plate 3.

Mini Potpourri Wreaths and Pomanders

CREATE one of these mini wreaths or pomanders to bring a breath of spring to any room in your home. Hang it on a door so that you will notice its scent when you enter the room, or put it in a sunny window where its fragrance will be released by the sun's warmth. You can use purchased or homemade potpourri for a cover, but, in either case, choose a potpourri in which the flowers have retained a good amount of color. For a romantic finishing touch, trim with dried rosebuds, ribbons, and streamers. Because this project is so simple and the results very rewarding, plan to make several for yourself and a few extra for gifts.

SUPPLIES
Potpourri: 3 cups for a wreath, 1 cup for a pomander ball
Whole rosebuds (optional)
7" heart-shaped Styrofoam wreath, or 3" Styrofoam ball
Tacky glue
Craft stick for spreading glue
Velvet or satin ribbon: 2 yards of ⅛" or ¼" for a wreath, 1 yard of ¼" or ½" for a pomander
Paper clip for hanging

MAKING A POTPOURRI WREATH OR POMANDER

1. Spread the potpourri in a pie plate.

2. *Wreath:* Cover the back and halfway up the sides of the wreath with an evenly applied coat of glue. Place the wreath in the plate of potpourri and press firmly. Turn the wreath over and cover the front and remaining side sections with glue. Once again, press it into the plate of potpourri. Dot any empty spaces with more glue and pack the potpourri in place to completely cover the wreath base, except for a spot where you can attach the bow.

Cut a 60" length from the 2 yards of ribbon and form it into four loops. Tie the remaining length of ribbon tightly around the middle of the loops, making a bow of eight loops. (See Figure 3-3.) Glue the bow to the top center of the wreath. This bow also looks pretty glued to the top of a pomander.

Pomander: Cover one half of the Styrofoam ball with an evenly applied coat of thick glue and roll it in the potpourri. Repeat on the other half, overlapping the glue between sections so that the ball will be completely covered except for a small space at the top to insert the hanger. Cut two 9¼" pieces of ribbon, spread glue on one side, and wrap them around the pomander at right angles to each other (see Figure 3-4).

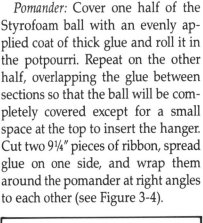

FIG. 3-4. *Wrap two pieces of ribbon around the pomander at right angles to each other.*

3. To attach a hanger to the wreath or ball, bend a paper clip into the shape of an S, apply glue to the small end, and push that end into the back center of the wreath or top center of the ball.

4. When the fragrance of the potpourri begins to fade, freshen it with a drop of scented oil.

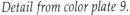

Detail from color plate 9.

FIG. 3-3. *Make four loops to start the bow, then tie the remaining ribbon around the center.*

Decorated Straw Hat

A DECORATED straw hat will add instant country ambience to your front door or a romantically feminine touch to a young girl's bedroom. The look you get will depend on the type of materials you choose to decorate the hat.

For a hat with true country flavor, start with a Spanish moss base, and add brightly colored dried flowers and a gingham, plaid, or pin-dot ribbon. For an old-fashioned, Victorian look, start with a German statice base; add baby's breath, rosebuds, and delicately colored flowers and finish with a satin or velvet bow. If you can't find just the right dried flowers, try ribbon roses; they're a beautiful alternative to the real thing and are available in most craft or sewing stores.

SUPPLIES

16-inch straw hat
Base material: Spanish moss or German statice
Hot-glue gun or tacky glue
1"-wide sponge brush for spreading glue
26" length of thin wire
Dried flower suggestions: American statice, baby's breath, strawflowers, rosebuds, cockscomb, globe amaranth
3 yards of 1½" decorative ribbon
Scissors

DECORATING A STRAW HAT

1. Begin by attaching the base material of your choice to the hat.

Spanish moss: Starting as close to the crown as possible, spread a 2½" band of glue evenly around the brim of the hat. Leave a 3" section unglued where the bow will be attached. Separate the moss into wide strands and gently press it in place around the band.

German statice: German statice is usually sold dried. If it is too brittle to handle, try misting it lightly with a spray bottle before you begin. If the statice appears matted or flattened, revive it by quickly immersing it in hot water; shake it to fluff it out. Allow the statice to dry before using it. Break the statice into 5" pieces. Starting at the rear of the crown and working toward the center top, begin gluing sprays of statice along the brim in one direction and as close to the crown as possible. When you get halfway around, start from the rear of the crown again and complete the other side, blending the statice in the middle. A hot-glue gun works well for attaching statice. To prevent burning your fingertips, hold the statice in place with an old, blunt-tipped knife or a craft stick while the glue dries. Apply a full base, but remember to leave a spot for attaching the bow.

2. Form 6" of wire into a loop and attach it to the center of the back brim for hanging. Before gluing the flowers to the base material, place them around the brim, hang the hat on a wall, and stand back to get a picture of how it will look. A symmetrical arrangement of flowers helps create an attractive finished product. When you are satisfied, begin attaching individual medium-size flowers by first dipping the stems in glue and then pressing them in place. Fill in with smaller flower heads and complete the design with a few sprigs of white or dyed baby's breath.

3. This method of making a bow will work with any ribbon, but it works best with crisp fabrics. Cut 1¾ yards of ribbon and a 20" length of thin wire. Form a 3" loop at one end of the ribbon, pinch the bottom of the loop between your thumb and forefinger and tightly wrap the wire twice around the ribbon, just above your fingers (Figure 3-5). Then make

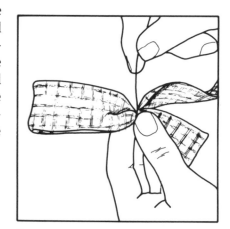

FIG. 3-5. *Make a loop with the ribbon and tightly wrap with wire.*

a second loop of ribbon the same size, slightly behind the first. Tightly wrap the wire in the same direction around both loops (Figure 3-6). Continue making 3″ loops, pointed upward, one behind the other, cinching each tightly to the others with wire. When you have used all the ribbon, you should have seven or eight loops. Snip off the excess wire.

Gently twist the loops to the side to make a full, circular bow (Figure 3-7).

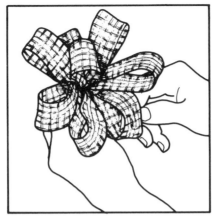

FIG. 3-7. *Gently bend the loops out for a fuller bow.*

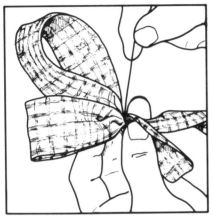

FIG. 3-6. *Make a second loop and wrap the end with wire.*

4. For streamers, cut one 18″ and one 21″ length of ribbon and cut a notch in one end of each. Slightly overlap the unnotched ends and glue them in place on the hat brim. Glue the bow over the streamers.

Detail from color plate 8.

Dried Apple Wreath with Cinnamon Hearts

THE traditional dried apple wreath is made even more interesting with the addition of three cinnamon-scented wooden hearts. The combination of the apple and cinnamon scents makes this a truly irresistible kitchen accessory.

Delicious apples work especially well in this wreath, as they dry to a rich, woody color. You should be able to find small wooden hearts at a craft store; if not, you can cut them from ¼" lattice. Cinnamon oil should be available at a pharmacy.

SUPPLIES
4 pounds of small apples
3 cookie sheets and a knife
3 small wooden hearts
Drill with ⅛" bit
Cinnamon oil
1½' of ⅛" satin ribbon
Wire coat hanger and pliers
1½ yards of 1½" ribbon for bow
Wire or twine for hanging

MAKING AN APPLE WREATH

1. Remove the stems from the apples, but do not peel or core them. Cut the apples into ⅛"-thick slices. (I like to slice the apples lengthwise because the slices have a pretty, almost heart shape, but you can cut them crosswise if you prefer.)

2. Place the apple slices on a lightly greased cookie sheet; do not overlap. Bake them in a 200-degree oven for three to five hours, turning every hour until dried; or you can bake them overnight in a 150-degree oven. The shape in which they will dry is unpredictable — some curl, others stay flat — but use them all.

3. If you are cutting your own wooden hearts, trace the pattern onto ¼" pine lattice (untreated), cut with a scroll saw, and drill a small hole at the top of each heart for the ribbon. If you are using purchased hearts, drill a small hole in the top of each one. Pour a small amount of cinnamon oil into a shallow dish or jar lid and soak the wooden hearts until they are saturated; there's no need to drain them. Cut the ⅛" satin ribbon into three different lengths and string it through each heart. Tie the three ribbons together at the top and set the hearts aside.

4. Remove the top (the hook) of the coat hanger. Form a 28" length of hanger wire into an 8" circle, leaving the ends open at the top. String the apples onto the wire, leaving a 1" space at each end of the wire. Using pliers, bend each end back into a U-shape and hook the ends together. Hang the wooden hearts from this section and add a bow (see step 3 under Decorated Straw Hat, page 56). Attach a wire or piece of twine to the top center of the wreath for hanging.

Detail from color plate 5.

Pattern for Wooden Hearts

Cut out three.

Stove-Top Simmer

WHEN it seems that there's never enough time in the day to keep up with all of life's demands, it helps to have something to soothe one's senses. Here's a recipe to make your whole house smell deliciously warm and inviting. But be prepared for complaints when it's discovered that you're not baking an apple pie. (My husband can sadly attest to the number of times his search for that elusive dessert has led him to the inedible potpourri on the stove.) When not simmering on the stove, this fragrant blend can be displayed in an open bowl or a pretty apothecary jar and enjoyed as a tabletop potpourri.

SUPPLIES
10 drops of cinnamon oil or apple spice oil
1 tablespoon of orrisroot powder or chips (optional)
2 cups of apple slices
1 cup of orange rind, cut into small pieces
1 cup of broken cinnamon sticks
3 whole nutmegs, broken
½ cup each of whole cloves, star anise, and allspice berries
¼ cup of bay leaves, broken

MAKING STOVE-TOP SIMMER

1. Dry the apple slices and orange rinds in a 200-degree oven as described in step 2 under Dried Apple Wreath on page 58; or, if you're not in a hurry, air-dry the apple slices by stringing them on a heavy thread and hanging them in a warm, dry spot (over a fireplace mantel or from a rafter). I keep a hanging wire mesh basket in my kitchen for drying the rinds of oranges, lemons, and limes. Strip them of their white inner layer, cut them into thin strips, and remember to stir them occasionally while they're drying. When the apples are dry, cut them into pieces.

2. Mix the cinnamon oil with the orrisroot. (If you are not using orrisroot, mix cinnamon oil with the dried apples and orange rinds; they will absorb and hold the fragrance.)

3. Blend the spices, fruit, and bay leaf together; then add the orrisroot mixture.

4. Add ½ cup of the apple spice blend to 3 cups of water, or wrap the mixture in a piece of cheesecloth, and simmer slowly. Add more water as needed. The mixture can be refrigerated and used again. If you have a tabletop potpourri burner, add 1 to 2 tablespoons of the blend to water and enjoy the fragrance in any room.

Apple Jack-o'-Lanterns

THE Irish have been credited with bringing the traditions of Halloween to America. According to Irish folklore, the legend of the jack-o'-lantern is said to have started when a surly Irishman named Jack was expelled from hell for tricking the devil. His spirit was doomed to wander the earth carrying a lantern to light his way. Fearing the arrival of his and others' evil spirits, the Irish would place candlelit hollowed-out turnips or potatoes in their windows. Although we don't take the warding off of evil spirits very seriously today, the older tradition is a charming divergence from our contemporary jack-o'-lanterns and worth reviving. Carve an apple instead of a pumpkin — it's not nearly as messy and will add a spooky glow to even the smallest corner of your room.

SUPPLIES
Largest apples you can find
Sharp paring knife and spoon
Felt-tip pen
Small candles

Detail from color plate 6.

MAKING APPLE JACK-O'-LANTERNS

1. Using a paring knife, cut a round piece from the top of each apple for a lid.

2. With the paring knife, cut along the inside of the apple, leaving at least ¼" of pulp attached to the skin. Scrape and scoop out the inside with a spoon.

3. Draw an outline of eyes, nose, and mouth on the apple with the marker and carefully carve out the features.

4. Carve a small hole in the bottom of each apple to serve as a candle holder if necessary.

Cornhusk Dolls

THE growing and harvesting of corn played a major part in the daily lives of the first settlers who came to America. From the Indians they learned the marvelous versatility of this once unknown crop. In addition to cooking it, they learned to pop it and to braid its husks into rugs, brooms, and baskets. At one time the Colonists even used corn kernels as a system of currency! October's husking bee — a time to celebrate and share in the harvest — turned into a much anticipated annual social event.

One of the most enduring and charming uses of corn was the crafting of cornhusk dolls. Even today, the natural beauty of these dolls endears them to collectors. Due to their extreme fragility, few of the early dolls have survived, but the tradition of creating them has been retained and passed down through the generations. This is still a popular craft in the southern highland regions of the United States.

This project can be made either with husks purchased from a craft store or with those dried from fresh corn. If you use fresh husks, save only the inner, finer-grained husks and the corn silk (for the hair). To dry the corn silk and husks, spread them between layers of newspaper or between two window screens and place them in the sun to dry. Drying should take about a week. When thoroughly dry, the husks will be light yellow and shriveled.

I prefer their natural golden color, but if you wish to add color to the husks, you can dye them with packaged fabric dyes. Mix 1 teaspoon of dye with 1 quart of very hot water. Pour the dye into a shallow pan and completely immerse the cornhusks. Soak the husks for at least five minutes, or until you get the shade you want. Blot the husks on a paper towel before using them.

Detail from color plate 2.

MAKING THE DOLL

1. Soak the husks about ten minutes to make them pliable. Do not leave husks soaking in water while you work, however, or they will turn a grayish color when dry. Remove the husks from the water and place them on paper towels or a terry towel. To keep them from drying out, cover them with a damp towel. Cut off the pointed ends to give the husks a flatter, more uniform size. Notice that the husks have a ribbed and a smooth side; always keep the smooth side of the husk turned to the outside.

2. Choose two fine-grained husks for the face and head and trim them to 3″ x 5″. Tightly tie the two 3″ x 5″ pieces together at one end. Invert the husks (knotted end to the inside), fan out each section, and wrap the husks tightly around a 1″ ball made from cotton or Styrofoam. Twist wire around the husks just under the ball to form a head and neck. The husks should extend 2″ to 3″ below the head in front and back. (See Figure 3-8.) (This will become the doll's

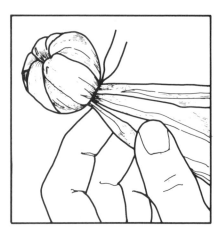

FIG. 3-8. *Wrap cornhusks around a small ball for the head.*

chest; a long skirt will take the place of the rest of her.)

3. To make the arms, roll a 7″ piece of medium-weight wire or pipe cleaner lengthwise in a 9″ x 2″ piece of husk and tie it in the middle with wire. There should be 1″ of husk extending beyond the wire at each end. To make the hands, fold this 1″ section back at each end, forming a loop, and secure it at the "wrist" with wire (Figure 3-9). The arms can be left as they are, or, for a fancier look, you

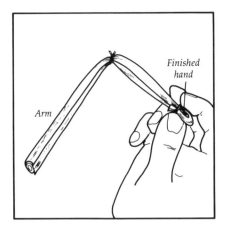

FIG. 3-9. *Make hands by folding a husk back and securing it with wire.*

FIG. 3-11. *Fill out the chest area with husks or cotton balls.*

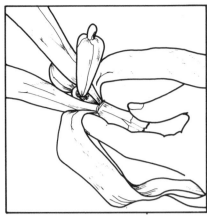

FIG. 3-13. *Attach husks around the waist and invert to form a skirt.*

can attach full sleeves. To make sleeves, cut two 3″ x 5″ sections of husk for each arm. Place one piece of husk on each side of the wrist, extending about 4½″ beyond the wrist. Wrap wire tightly around the wrist and the ends of the husk pieces. Then invert the sleeve, shaping it over the arm so there are no gaps (use glue if necessary) and wire the sleeve to the top of the arm. (See Figure 3-10.) Repeat on the other side.

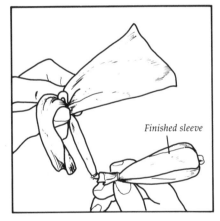

FIG. 3-10. *Attach the husk at the wrist, then invert it to make a sleeve.*

4. Slide the arms between the front and back chest areas just beneath the neck; then stuff and shape the upper body cavity with husks or cotton balls. (See Figure 3-11.) For a blouse, cut two 2″ x 5″ pieces of husk. Place the middle of one on each shoulder and crisscross the strips in the front and back. Secure the ends of the

blouse strips and make a waist by wrapping wire around the doll under the chest stuffing (Figure 3-12).

FIG. 3-12. *Crisscross cornhusk strips across the chest and secure the ends with wire.*

5. For a full skirt, cut at least six 7½″ x 5″ sections of husks. Raise the doll's arms and place the husks around the waist on all sides; the husks should extend from over the head of the doll to just below the waist. (See Figure 3-13.) Wrap wire tightly around the ends of these husks at the waistline. Invert the husks and fold them down to form a skirt.

6. Trim the husks evenly along the bottom edge and wrap a string loosely around the middle of the skirt to hold it in place (if the string is too

tight, it will leave an indentation). (See Figure 3-14.) Allow the doll to dry in place overnight. When the doll is completely dry, remove the string and glue closed any obvious gaps in the skirt.

7. Draw very simple half-moon-shaped eyes on the face with a fine felt-tip pen. In keeping with the natural look of the doll, fashion hair from corn silk, flax, wool, or jute twine. Use your imagination to give your doll her own personality with finishing touches such as a miniature bouquet of dried flowers, a straw hat, ribbons in the hair, or a baby to cradle. Or cut a pair of cornhusk wings and transform her into a Christmas angel to place on the family tree.

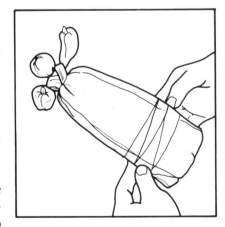

FIG. 3-14. *Wrap string loosely around the skirt until dry.*

Harvest Wreath

TO AMERICAN pioneers, a cornhusk wreath symbolized an abundant harvest. Today this golden-hued wreath is a pleasing alternative to the simple clusters of Indian corn adorning many front entrances in the fall.

SUPPLIES
10" straw wreath base
3" length of thin wire
Cornhusks (one 6-ounce package)
Paper towels
Scissors
Florist's U pins or picks
Dried yarrow, strawflowers, or similar dried flowers
Tacky glue
1 yard of 1½" ribbon

MAKING THE WREATH

1. Form the wire into a loop and attach it to the back of the wreath base for hanging. This will establish the top and the starting point.

2. Soak the husks in warm water for about ten minutes to make them more pliable. Blot each one dry on a paper towel before beginning to work with it.

3. Tear or cut 8" lengths of husks into ½"-wide strips. Fold these strips in half and group seven or eight together to form a cluster. Pinch the ends of the cluster together, hold them in place on the wreath base, and push a pin over them. Continue to attach clusters in a clockwise direction around the base. Each cluster of husks should cover the base of the previous cluster. (See Figure 3-15.) Continue the layering process until the entire surface of the wreath is covered and the desired fullness is achieved.

4. For a color accent, glue dried sprigs of yarrow or strawflowers around the wreath. Or make three 5" bows by first cutting 1 yard of ribbon into three 12" pieces. Form each piece into a circle, overlapping the ends 1". Pinch the ribbon together in the center and wrap a wire pick tightly around the middle of each bow. Attach the bows to the wreath with wire picks at three different points to further highlight the design.

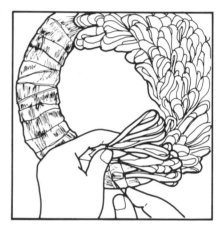

FIG. 3-15. *Each cluster should cover the base of the one before it.*

Detail from color plate 5.

Spicy Fruit Pomander Balls

POMANDER balls have been used for centuries to add a pleasant fragrance to one's surroundings. Early settlers used clove-studded fruits to mask unpleasant cooking odors and the strong smell of tobacco or wood smoke in their small kitchens. Victorian women hung floral pomanders (see Mini Potpourri Wreaths and Pomanders, page 55) in closets or tucked them into drawers to dispel musty odors and repel moths.

Today pomanders are as popular as ever. For year-round use they serve as natural room fresheners. When hung on the Christmas tree, they fill the air with a pungent holiday fragrance. To make the pomanders in this chapter, look for firm, thin-skinned fruits, free of blemishes.

SUPPLIES

Curing mixture (enough to make about four): 8 tablespoons cinnamon, 1 tablespoon allspice, 1 tablespoon nutmeg, 2 tablespoons powdered orrisroot
Small paper clips for hooks
Ribbon or lace for hanging
Firm, medium-size fruits: apples, oranges, limes, lemons
Knitting needle, medium-size nail, or toothpick for piercing fruit (optional)
Whole cloves (1½ to 2 ounces per pomander)

MAKING FRUIT POMANDER BALLS

1. Blend the curing mixture in a flat-bottomed bowl and set it aside.

2. If you plan to hang your pomander balls, prepare them for hanging in one of two ways. One method is to bend a small paper clip into the shape of an S and push the smaller of the ends into the fruit until only about ¼" is visible at the top (Figure 3-16). This will serve as a hook. Another method is to bind the pomander with ribbon, using this as a means for hanging. If you prefer to hang it with ribbon, leave two clove-free paths the width of your ribbon, forming perpendicular circumferences around the ball (see Figure 3-4, page 55).

3. Hold the fruit firmly in your hand and push the cloves into the rind. When using thick-skinned fruit (such as limes or lemons), or when the children are helping, you might find it helpful to pierce the rind first with a knitting needle or nail, and then insert the clove into the hole. It is not necessary to follow any pattern; just cover the entire surface, inserting the cloves about ⅛" apart. The fruit will shrink and the cloves will come together when the pomander has dried and hardened.

4. Roll the clove-studded fruit in the curing mixture until it is completely covered.

5. Put the pomanders in a bowl and place it in a cool, dark, dry place, such as a kitchen cupboard or closet. Do not crowd the balls in the bowl; there should be room around each for air to circulate. Depending on weather conditions and the size of the fruit, pomanders will take from two to four weeks to dry and harden. Inspect and turn them from time to time. The fruit feels hard and firm when completely dried. The process can be speeded up by partially drying the pomanders in a 200-degree oven for several hours before air-drying them.

6. After the pomanders have dried, remove them from the bowl and tap off any excess powder. Any extra curing mixture can be saved in a plastic bag for future use. Decorate the pomanders with ribbons, bows, or lace.

7. The spicy fragrance will last a long time but will eventually begin to fade. Don't discard the pomander! The fragrance can be restored by dipping the pomander in boiling water, then rolling it in the reserved curing mixture. Remove any excess powder and hang the pomander to dry.

Detail from color plate 6.

FIG. 3-16. *Push the smaller end of the S-hook into the fruit.*

Spicy Cookie Ornaments

BECAUSE of their tempting aroma and gingerbread appearance, you might have to fend off some hungry "cookie monsters" when you bake these ornaments. Unfortunately, they cannot be eaten. But pass out the cutters anyway, and get ready to create much more than cookies (this is a project the children will enjoy getting their hands into). Once they are finished, you'll find lots of ways to use these spicy ornaments. String them with yarn and hang them on your tree, in windows, or anywhere you want to savor the scent of Christmas. Or cut them into the shape of hearts and gingerbread men, trim with white paint "icing," and glue them onto your Christmas wreaths. This recipe will make twelve to fourteen 3" "cookies."

When the holidays are over, gather up the ornaments, broken pieces and all, and use them as the base for a stove-top potpourri. Just drop them in a pot of water, add a cinnamon stick and a few cloves, and simmer (adding water as needed). Within minutes your kitchen will be filled with an enticing aroma reminiscent of Grandmother's cookies hot from the oven.

SUPPLIES
1 cup of applesauce
1-1¼ cups of ground cinnamon or a combination of ground cinnamon, cloves, nutmeg, and allspice
Wax paper, cookie cutters, rolling pin
Cookie sheets, flat metal spatula
White acrylic paint and a small brush (optional)
Yarn, thin ribbon, thin wire, or Christmas ornament hangers

MAKING THE ORNAMENTS

1. Mix the applesauce and cinnamon or spices until they are well blended. Knead the mixture until it is the consistency of clay. Add more cinnamon, if necessary, to reach the right consistency. Chill.

2. Place the dough between two layers of wax paper and roll it out to a thickness of ¼". Cut with cookie cutters or a knife. If desired, pierce a design into the surface with a toothpick, then poke a small hole in the top of each cookie for hanging. Or form a piece of thin wire into a small loop, twist the loop closed near the bottom, and flare the ends slightly to prevent the hook from slipping out. (See Figure 3-17.) Carefully push the flared ends into the top edge of the ornament; the wire will be set when the ornament is dry. Transfer the cookies to a lightly greased (I use a spray) cookie sheet.

FIG. 3-17. *A loop of wire with flared ends is pushed into the edge of the ornament.*

3. Set the oven at 150 degrees and slowly bake the ornaments. To prevent the edges from curling, turn the cookies every thirty minutes until they are dry. Depending on the thickness of the dough, drying will take from three to four hours (the cookies will feel very hard when thoroughly dry). If you prefer, you can air-dry them on a cookie sheet. This will take about five days; turn each cookie daily.

4. When the cookies are dry, leave them plain or paint on an icing trim. String thin ribbon through the hole and hang them wherever you like.

Detail from color plate 6.

Potato Prints

POTATO printing is a fun, inexpensive, and personal way to decorate wrapping paper, party napkins, or Christmas card envelopes. Ordinary paper sandwich bags can be transformed into festive gift bags with a potato, some red and green paint, and bright holiday ribbons to top them off. Once Mom or Dad has done the carving, children will enjoy designing and stamping, and making their own creations.

SUPPLIES
Firm medium-size potatoes
Paper towels
Felt-tip pen (fine point), paring knife
Acrylic paints, paper plate, small paintbrushes
Plain white shelf paper, paper sandwich bags, brown wrapping paper, or envelopes for stamping

Detail from color plate 6.

MAKING POTATO PRINTS

1. Cut a potato in half and blot the cut end of the potato on a paper towel. Using a fine felt-tip pen, draw a design on the cut end of the potato (see the patterns). Words, letters, and numbers must be written and carved in reverse. Keep the designs simple. Hold the knife perpendicular to the surface of the potato and cut the edges of the design about ½″ deep. Remove the background a little at a time until your design stands in relief. (See Figure 3-18.) Blot it on a paper towel to remove some of the excess moisture.

2. Put a little paint on a paper plate. Brush a thin layer of paint onto the raised stamp design with a small paintbrush. More than one color can be printed at a time (as on the holly-and-berries design), but always use a separate brush for each color. Test your stamp on a piece of scrap paper to determine the right amount of paint and pressure to apply to achieve the look you want. When you are satisfied, press the stamp firmly on the surface you wish to decorate and then lift it straight up to prevent smearing the edges. You should get two to three printings from each paint application. Since the potato will eventually shrivel, plan on doing all your printing in one day, if possible. If necessary, however, the potato stamp can be kept in a bowl of water overnight in the refrigerator.

FIG. 3-18. *Cut away the background until the design stands in relief.*

Patterns for Potato Prints

4
Stenciling for the Home

STENCILING — a method of painting designs through cut-out patterns — was originally developed as a method to decorate trays, chairs, boxes, and other household items with greater speed and uniformity. It was most popular in America between 1775 and 1860. During this period, people used the technique extensively in their homes to imitate the look of expensive, imported wallpaper, embroidered fabrics, and Oriental rugs, bringing color and design to otherwise plain, drab rooms. Often the stenciling was done by itinerant house painters using paints derived from natural powdered products; the local red, green, and yellow earth clays, mixed in skimmed milk or buttermilk, made excellent bases for their paint. Some symbolism was evident in their patterns (willows were associated with immortality, the pineapple stood for hospitality, hearts and bells suggested joy), but for the most part designs were chosen for their ornamental value.

This early stenciling, when first done, often looked opaque and one-dimensional. With the passage of time, however, the stenciling became worn and faded, inadvertently taking on a softer, more three-dimensional look. It is that shaded, subtle appearance that is very popular with stencilers and decorators today, and it is easy to obtain when you use the proper technique.

Stenciling continued to be a popular method of home decoration through the mid-nineteenth century. Following the development and refinement of the silk-screening process, use of the craft began to wane. The availability of mass-produced linoleums and preprinted wallpapers made it unnecessary to decorate homes by hand, and stenciling was relegated to utilitarian purposes such as sign making and lettering.

Stenciling has been rediscovered, however, and is being used everywhere to add a touch of charm and personality to today's country, traditional, and even contemporary homes. Because no specific artistic talents are necessary to stencil, anyone can easily master this inexpensive decorating technique. Not only in this chapter, but throughout this book, stenciling is employed to help you create unique, practical, and decorative items for your home. Almost anything that can be painted or printed can be stenciled. So practice the techniques described and then begin to enjoy this truly versatile craft. You'll be amazed at how quickly you can learn to stencil and, in doing so, give a room a distinctive, one-of-a-kind look. But be forewarned: Stenciling can be habit forming. To quote an artist friend with a charming and beautiful home, "If it stands still long enough, I'll stencil it!"

Making and Using Stencils

Once you have taken the time to learn and perfect the technique of cutting your own stencils, you will be glad you did. The dollar savings alone are worth the investment of time required to learn this skill. But beyond that, with this technique in hand, the creative possibilities are endless. You can adapt designs from wallpaper and fabric to repeat elsewhere in your room on floors, walls, tablecloths, pillows, or furniture — or design your own patterns. With a little practice, the technique of stencil cutting is easy to master.

Stencils used by early decorators were usually cut from heavy paper that was oiled on both sides to prevent the paint from seeping through. These stencils were fragile and became worn after repeated use. I recommend using frosted Mylar, a durable material that is available at most art or drafting supply stores. (If Mylar is unavailable, use clear acetate.)

Stencils used in this chapter are cut in one of two ways: Either the entire design is traced on and cut from a single piece of Mylar (*full-design stencil*); or the design is divided by color, each color to be traced and cut on a separate piece of Mylar (*color-separated stencils*). The pros and cons of both methods are described in the following paragraphs. After you have made and used both, you will be better able to decide which method you prefer to use when designing your own stencils.

The primary advantage of the full-design stencil is that it is easier to cut an entire design from a single piece of Mylar. When using this type of stencil, the bridges (sections of Mylar between the cut-out areas that hold the stencil together) will remain unpainted on your finished design. In most cases, this poses no problem and doesn't detract from the finished look. When using more than one color on this stencil, you must isolate the different-colored areas with masking tape to prevent the paint on one section of the design from getting on a section of another color. (To avoid pulling off any paint when you remove tape from a painted area, take away some of its stickiness by pressing the tape on cloth before using it.) You can use small pieces of paper or Mylar instead of tape, but hold them firmly in place while you stencil.

Cutting color-separated stencils is more time consuming and necessitates extra steps to ensure proper alignment of the different stencils. It does, however, preclude the need to mask off areas while stenciling different colors, and it eliminates unpainted areas left by the bridges of a full-design stencil. To simplify the projects in this chapter, I have avoided using color-separated stencils whenever possible, but when certain design elements in a pattern require color-separated stencils, I have already separated them and numbered them in the order of their use.

Acrylic paint is recommended for all the stenciled projects in this book. Acrylics blend well, dry quickly, and are water soluble, allowing for soap-and-water cleanup. (Since they do dry quickly, place only a *small* amount of paint on your palette at one time.) For stenciling on a fabric that is to be washed periodically, use acrylic fabric paint.

STENCIL BRUSHES

When choosing brushes for stenciling, as for any type of decorative painting, it is wise to buy the best-quality brush you can afford. I prefer to use a natural, rather than a synthetic, bristle brush. Natural bristles retain paint better and are more flexible, to permit beautiful shading. The bristles of a stencil brush are all cut the same length, forming a circular flat surface for painting. They are available in a variety of sizes (the sizes are given in numbers — the higher the number, the larger the brush) and can be used on hard and soft surfaces. Stencil brushes for painting only on fabric are available, but they are not a necessity. To stencil a small area in a design, I like to use a natural-bristle bright brush. Unlike

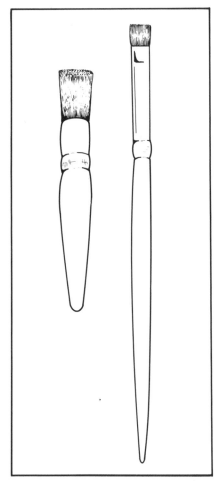

FIG. 4-1. *Stencil brush (left) and natural-bristle bright brush (right).*

the bristles of a stencil brush, which are round and blunt-ended, brights have narrow, square-ended bristles and a sharp, flat edge, making them ideal for getting into hard-to-reach areas. (See Figure 4-1.)

Plan to use one brush for each color of your design. If you don't have enough brushes for a given project and find it necessary to reuse a brush, wash and dry it completely (a blow dryer helps) before using it again. Brushes must be thoroughly dry before they are dipped into paint, as any moisture left in a brush can cause the paint to smear.

TRACING A STENCIL

Full-design stencil: Cut a piece of Mylar 1" larger on all sides than the design you wish to copy. This margin will allow you more space to move your brush without worrying about marring your project by running off the edge of the stencil (it also adds strength to the stencil). Place the Mylar, frosted side up (this side takes pencil marks well), over the design. Tape it in place to prevent shifting. (Since Mylar is semitransparent, the design will be visible and can be easily traced.) Trace all parts of the design with a fine felt-tip pen or a sharp pencil. (See Figure 4-2.)

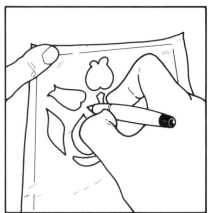

FIG. 4-2. *Tracing a pattern onto Mylar.*

Color-separated stencils: Study your design and decide how many colors you want to use and where on the design they will be located. Cut as many equal-size pieces of blank Mylar as colors you have chosen (remember to allow the 1" margin around the design). For example, a pattern that has pink flowers and green leaves will require two pieces. Tape one piece of Mylar, frosted side up, over your pattern. Trace all the design areas of the first (most predominant) color with a solid line. Then trace all or parts of the other color areas of the design with broken lines. These broken lines will allow you to align each stencil with the others. Label the first piece of Mylar stencil A and note the color you will be using with it. Tape the second piece of Mylar over the first, making sure the corners are aligned. Trace all design elements of the second color with a solid line and, once again, all or parts of the other colors with broken lines. Label this one stencil B and note the color. Repeat this process until all colors of the design have been traced.

CUTTING A STENCIL

To cut a stencil, place a Mylar tracing, shiny side up (the blade will move more easily), on a pane of glass. Hold your knife as you would a pencil; be careful, however, not to lean it to the side. Using a firm, steady pressure (don't press too hard or the tip of the blade will snap), cut along the lines of the design. (See Figure 4-3.) Always cut toward you. Start in the center of the design and work toward the edges, cutting out the smaller design areas first. Use one continuous cutting stroke until you reach a corner, then stop and, without lifting your knife, turn the Mylar in the direction of the uncut design and continue cutting and turning the Mylar until that part of the design is removed. Repeat for the remaining sections.

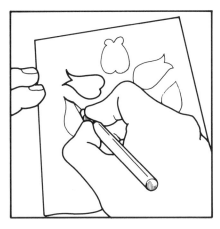

FIG. 4-3. *Cutting a stencil with an X-acto knife.*

When you are cutting a large circle or curve, hold the knife still and turn just the Mylar. Small dots or circles can be punched out with a large needle, the edges on the reverse side trimmed with small scissors and smoothed with very fine sandpaper. To cut fine lines and stems, cut one side with an X-acto knife, then use small scissors to pare the stencil opening to the desired width. It is important to remember not to lift your knife while cutting but to let the hand holding the Mylar do the work. This will ensure sharp, clean edges, and the smoother the edges, the more attractive your finished stenciling will look.

A sharp blade is essential for clean cuts; when cutting a large stencil, you might find it necessary to change your blade before completing the design. If you run outside a line or cut across a bridge, apply a small piece of transparent tape to each side of the Mylar and cut that part again.

Practice stenciling your design on scrap paper before starting your project. This will allow you to check the accuracy of your cutting and the alignment of color-separated stencils. You will also get an idea of how the colors you have chosen will look together.

HOW TO STENCIL

1. Place your stencil on the surface you are going to decorate and secure it in place with tape. If you are using one stencil for the entire design, mask off the areas of a different color from the one you are starting with.

2. Stenciling requires very little paint, so place only 1 or 2 teaspoons of paint on your palette (you can use a small paper plate). Next to your paint place a stack of three or four folded paper towels.

3. Dip only the *tip* of the brush's bristles into the paint. Work the paint up into the bristles and remove excess paint by dabbing the brush on the stack of paper towels. (See Figure 4-4.) This step might seem to be a waste of paint, but the most important thing to remember when stenciling is: *Use a very dry brush.* When you apply the paint, it should feel almost powdery. Too much paint will result in an opaque, painted look; it will also cause the paint to seep under the stencil. Depending on the size of your stencil, you should be able to do several stencil designs before reloading your brush.

FIG. 4-4. *Working the paint into the brush.*

4. There are primarily two ways to work your brush: stippling and the circular motion.

Stippling: Hold the brush perpendicular to the stencil and use an up-and-down, dabbing motion to apply the paint through the stencil opening. Always work from the outside to the inside of the stencil opening to prevent paint from bleeding under the edges. Stippling can be used on any surface, but it is especially suited to stenciling on fabric, as the up-and-down motion helps to work the paint into the weave of the material.

Circular motion: Beginning at the outside edges of the stencil opening, apply a light layer of paint, using a circular clockwise brush motion all around the opening. Repeat this process, going counterclockwise around the opening, alternating directions and working toward the center, until you are finished. (See Figure 4-5.) Never stencil from the center of an opening toward the edge because the paint will seep under the stencil, causing ragged edges. To ensure sharp, crisp edges, remember always to use a dry brush and keep the stencil as close to the surface as possible by pressing down the edges of the stencil opening closest to the area you are stenciling.

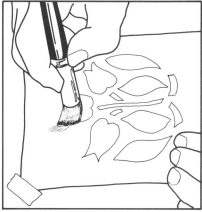

FIG. 4-5. *Begin at the edge of the opening and work toward the center.*

5. To give the design a faded, shaded, or three-dimensional look, leave a lighter area in the center of each design. Color intensity should be built up gradually by applying several thin coats of the same color, a darker shade of the first color, or a different color altogether. Make sure the first application is dry before applying the next layer.

6. Since acrylic paint dries quickly, you should be able to lift the stencil immediately after painting — unless you have loaded your brush with too much paint. If there is a stencil B for your design, remove stencil A; then place stencil B on top of your already stenciled area, align the pattern lines, tape it in place, and apply the next color.

7. Don't get discouraged if your designs are not absolutely perfect. Remember, stenciling is a handicraft and should not look machine-made — slight imperfections are part of its charm. But if you are stenciling on a painted base and wish to clean up some ragged edges or imperfections, dip a brush in the base color and make the necessary corrections.

CLEANING UP

Stencils: Place the stencil on a flat cloth or a stack of paper towels. Dip a stencil brush into rubbing alcohol. Gently rotate the bristles in a circular motion along the cut edges of the stencil (just as if you were stenciling). This action will help loosen the dried paint from the stencil. When most of the paint has been removed, dip a soft cloth in the alcohol and gently rub to remove the final traces. Let the stencil dry and store it flat. With proper care, your stencils will last forever.

Brushes: To extend the life of your brushes, clean them immediately after use. Never leave them soaking in water or other solvents. Wash them with a mild soap, then rinse. To remove any remaining paint, dip them into rubbing alcohol and wipe them on paper towels until there are no traces of paint on the towel. Shape the bristles and store the brushes vertically, bristles up.

Stenciled Tulip Pillow

IN COLONIAL America, stenciling on cloth, usually homespun cotton or linen, was a commonly used method of duplicating the look of expensive hand-embroidered and appliquéd fabrics. To the early-nineteenth-century woman with little extra time or money, it was the perfect way to embellish tablecloths, curtains, bed hangings, and counterpanes with brightly colored designs in half the time it took to embroider them.

Tulips, a symbol of faith, were a favorite motif of the folk artist, particularly among the Pennsylvania Dutch, and can be found on everything from paper cuttings to quilts. The tulip design for this pillow is derived from an 1840 appliquéd piece; you can enhance the stenciling and give it an appliquéd appearance by quilting around the design. The stencil is given as a half pattern; turn it around and repeat it on the other side for the complete design.

Once you have seen how simple it is to stencil on fabric, you can add to your decor with stenciled curtains, tablecloths, napkins ... but why stop there? Decorate your wardrobe as well with a stenciled scarf, bag, or T-shirt.

NOTE: I have used all-purpose acrylic paint for this project. If you are stenciling something that will be washed periodically, use a color-fast paint made especially for fabric (such as Fab-Tex by Stencil Ease).

SUPPLIES
14″ x 28″ piece of medium-weight white cotton fabric
Measuring tape, scissors
Tailor's chalk pencil
7″ x 12″ sheet of Mylar, X-acto knife, pane of glass, pencil
Wax paper, masking tape
Acrylic paint (Folk Art colors: Bluebell, Clover, Cherokee Rose)
Three stencil brushes
Paper plate, paper towels
14″-square piece each of quilt batting and muslin (optional)
Needle, straight pins, white thread
12-ounce bag of fiberfill

MAKING THE STENCILED PILLOW

1. Wash the cotton fabric to remove sizing and allow for shrinkage. Dry and press until wrinkle-free. Fold the fabric in half across the width and cut it along the fold line. Use tailor's chalk to draw a 12″ square on one piece, allowing 1″ extra on all sides for a seam allowance. Find the exact center of the square and mark it with a dot; draw a center guideline from top to bottom.

2. This design is cut as a full-design stencil. Tape the Mylar over the pattern on page 73, allowing a 1″ margin on all sides, and trace (transfer the center mark and the dotted centerline). Place the stencil on a pane of glass and cut it out with an X-acto knife.

3. Cut a 12″ square of wax paper to serve as a blotter. On a hard, flat surface, tape or tack the cotton over the wax paper, keeping the fabric as taut as possible. Center the stencil on the fabric by aligning the center dot and centerline on each and tape in place.

The tulips and the centers of the small flowers will be stenciled first in Bluebell; mask off all nearby openings of a different color. With an almost-dry brush, stencil, using the up-and-down stippling technique to force the paint into the weave of the fabric. Since the color may fade slightly after repeated washings, build layers of color gradually until you have sufficient depth and richness. To avoid a demarcation line, don't stencil along the centerline of the tulips; this area will be completed later. Stencil the stems and leaves Clover (mask the surrounding areas). Stencil the small flowers Cherokee Rose. Remove the stencil and position it on the other half of the pillow, overlapping the stencil opening slightly onto the stenciled half. Repeat the preceding steps to complete the design. Remove the stencil and carefully blend the paint at the center of the top and bottom tulips.

(Text continues on next page.)

Detail from color plate 7.

4. Allow the stenciling to dry and cure thoroughly — for at least twenty-four hours. Then, to set the paint, place a clean cloth over the design and press for about a minute with a warm (350-degree), dry iron. Turn the cloth over and press on the other side for one minute. The pillow cover can be hand-washed in cold water; never dry-clean because cleaning fluids tend to dissolve acrylic paints.

5. If you wish to quilt, lay the stenciled pillow top over the batting, with the muslin underneath. Baste the three layers together from the center to the corners. Then, starting in the middle of the design and working toward the edges, sew through all three layers, using tiny running stitches. Quilt as close as possible to the outside edge of the design lines (you will be outlining the pattern). Remove the basting when you have finished and trim the edges of all the layers to match.

6. If desired, you can sew a ruffle or a contrasting colored piping or strip of fabric at the seam line on the pillow front before it is attached to the back. Then pin the pillow front to back, right sides together, edges matching. Sew along the seam, keeping a 1" seam allowance on all sides. Leave a 4" opening along the bottom edge for turning and stuffing. Clip the corners. Turn the pillowcase right side out and press it gently. Stuff the pillow with fiberfill; then sew the opening closed.

Stenciled Tulip Pillow Half Pattern

STEM AND LEAVES —
Clover

Centerline

TULIPS AND CENTER
OF SMALL FLOWERS —
Bluebell

Center point ——+—

SMALL FLOWERS —
Cherokee Rose

Stenciled
Floorcloth

SUPPLIES
1 yard of 56″ No. 8 or No. 10 unprimed cotton duck canvas (available at art supply stores)
Newspapers
Flat white latex wall paint (primer)
Paint roller
Plastic wrap or bag for storing roller
Tack cloth
Yardstick, pencil, masking tape, scissors
Quick-drying glue, clothespins (optional)
Acrylic paint (Folk Art colors: Bluebell, Cherokee Rose, Clover, Honey Comb)
Four stencil brushes
14″ x 14″ sheet of Mylar, X-acto knife, pane of glass
Paper plate, paper towels
Satin-finish polyurethane varnish, wide brush
Fine-grit sandpaper

FLOORCLOTHS — rugs made of painted canvas — were popular in America during the mid-eighteenth through the nineteenth century. Just as stenciling took the place of expensive wallpaper, floorcloths served as a substitute for imported Oriental rugs. Though few floorcloths have survived the ravages of time (and their fall from fashion), many have been captured for posterity in the paintings of that period. Originally they were hand-painted, often to imitate marble or in geometric tile-like or checkered patterns. During the late eighteenth and early nineteenth centuries, the designs became more elaborate and stenciling replaced hand-painting as a quick and efficient method of repeating patterns.

Even with the myriad floor covering choices available today, floorcloths have been rediscovered as a welcome alternative to conventional rugs. Made with traditional folk art colors and patterns, they are a great way to add a touch of authenticity to a period home. But they're not only for vintage homes. You can enhance any room by adapting a design motif from a fabric or wallpaper pattern and repeating it on a floorcloth. The inspiration for my sun room's "contemporary-country" floorcloth (the pattern included here) came from a dhurrie rug in my living room. The design ties the two rooms together beautifully, but since the sun room gets more use and is exposed to the elements, a floorcloth is a more practical floor covering. They're wonderful in the kitchen, too, as stains and spills can be easily removed with a damp cloth.

So give it a try — you don't have to be a Picasso to paint this canvas! Just read through the basic instructions, then use either the patterns included or purchase precut stencils — or let your imagination be your guide in designing your own one-of-a-kind canvas carpet.

Detail from color plate 7.

PREPARING THE CANVAS

1. Iron the canvas to remove all wrinkles.

2. Lay the canvas on a flat, newspaper-covered surface while priming, preferably outdoors (but not in direct sunlight) to dissipate the fumes and shorten drying time. Using a paint roller, apply three coats of latex primer, two on the top of the canvas and one on the bottom. Press firmly so that the nap of the roller presses the paint into the weave of the canvas, overlapping your strokes to cover the cloth completely. Allow the first coat to dry thoroughly (two to four hours) before doing the next. To eliminate the need for cleaning the roller between coats, wrap it in plastic wrap or a large plastic food-storage bag. When the floorcloth is dry, wipe it with a tack cloth to remove grit and apply the next coat. Then turn it over and prime the bottom. The canvas will shrink somewhat as it dries. Don't be concerned if the edges become puckered (caused by shrinkage when drying) or frayed; they will be cut off or hemmed in a later step.

3. Measure and mark a 33" x 52" rectangle in the approximate middle of the canvas, leaving a margin on all four sides to allow for fraying as you work or in case you want to hem the floorcloth.

4. The varnish that will be applied as a finishing step will seal the cut edges and prevent them from fraying, so hemming is not necessary. But if you prefer a hem, trim the edges of the cloth to an even width, fold them under along the perimeter line, and miter the corners. Crease the hem and glue it in place with quick-drying glue. Press the edges with the back of a spoon or a rolling pin to seal the glue. Hold the mitered corners down with spring-loaded clothespins or a heavy weight until the glue is dry.

5. There are two ½" stripes around the border of the floorcloth, one on each side of the border design (See Figure 4-7). To establish the painting guidelines for the stripes, measure in from the perimeter line (or hemmed edge) and draw a light pencil line all around the floorcloth at the following distances: 1¾" and 2¼" (blue stripe), 5¾" and 6¼" (rose stripe). Between the stripes there is a 3½" space.

6. Divide the center section of the floorcloth equally from one end to the other and mark it with a light pencil line; then divide it into thirds, making six equal-size blocks. Intersect lines from opposite corners of each block to find the exact center of each; mark with a light pencil dot.

STENCILING THE DESIGN

1. The narrow bands of color flanking both sides of the floral border are done quickly and neatly by masking off each stripe with tape before stenciling. For a straight, clean edge, take care while masking and press the tape firmly along the pencil lines with your finger as you paint to prevent the paint from seeping under it. For sharp corners, overlap the tape and trim with an X-acto knife (Figure 4-6). Mask the blue stripe by placing masking tape along the 1¾" line and the 2¼" line (leaving a ½" stripe between the tape). Using the circular brush technique, stencil between the tape with Bluebell. Allow the paint to dry completely, then carefully remove the tape. If any seepage has occurred, cover it up with white primer. Then place tape along the 5¾" and 6¼" lines. Using the circular technique, stencil with Cherokee Rose. Allow the paint to dry, then carefully remove the tape. Correct any seepage with the white primer.

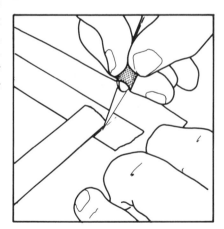

FIG. 4-6. *Overlap and trim the masking tape at the corner.*

2. All the floral designs will be cut as full-design stencils. Trace each design onto the Mylar; transfer the center marks to stencils C and D (pages 78-79). Cut the four stencils apart, leaving a 1" margin around each one. Remember to mask off the areas of a different color to prevent paint spatters.

3. Refer to the stencil patterns for color suggestions and to Figure 4-7 as a guide to design placement. The stencil A design will be repeated twelve times around the border. Begin by stenciling it once in each corner. Find the midpoint of each end of the floorcloth and stencil it again. Find the midpoint of each side and stencil. Now, *on the sides only*, find the midpoint between each corner and the middle design and stencil again. The stencil B design also will be repeated twelve times around the border. Center and stencil it to alternate with each stencil A design.

4. Using the center marks on the stencils and on the floorcloth as guides, position stencil C in the upper left corner block and stencil D in the upper right corner block and tape them in place. Since each design uses variations of the same colors, you can stencil them simultaneously. Allow the white of the floorcloth to show through at the center of each flower, if desired. Turn the stencils over and stencil the designs on opposite sides of the cloth in the next row of blocks. Then turn the stencils over once more, switch sides again, and stencil the last row.

FINISHING

1. Remove the margin (on an unhemmed floorcloth) by cutting along the penciled perimeter line with sharp scissors.

2. Varnish will preserve your floorcloth and prevent the edges from fraying; use at least three thin coats of clear polyurethane varnish on the painted side only. Before varnishing, let the paint dry thoroughly, for at least one day. If you varnish before the paint is completely dry, it might streak. First, erase all pencil marks and wipe the canvas with a tack cloth. Then apply the first coat of varnish with a wide brush, overlapping your brush strokes to ensure even coverage and running the brush along the cut edges to seal them. Let each coat dry about twenty-four hours before applying the next. Sand lightly between coats, wipe the floorcloth with a tack cloth, and apply the next coat.

3. Your floorcloth can be mopped with soap and water. For storage, roll it in a wide roll, stenciled side out. Never fold it. NOTE: If slipping becomes a problem, glue a thin sheet of foam to the back or spray the back with StaPut (liquid rubber in a can).

FIG. 4-7. *Floorcloth design layout.*

Floorcloth Stencils

STENCIL A

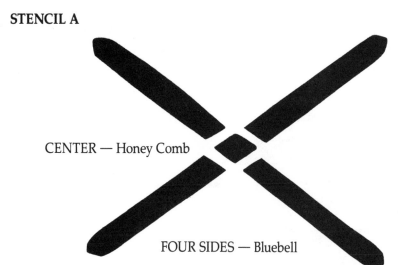

CENTER — Honey Comb

FOUR SIDES — Bluebell

STENCIL B

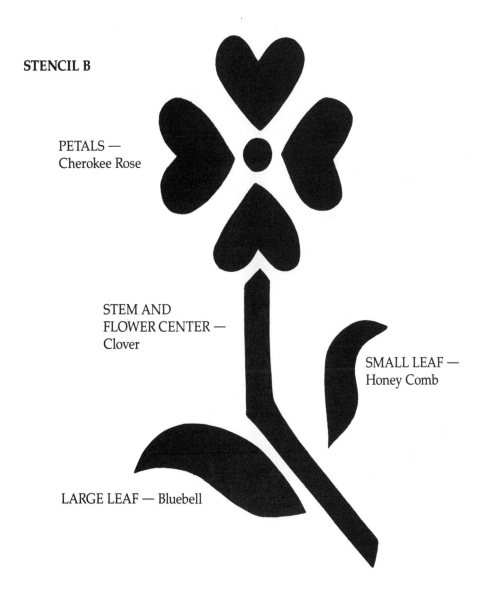

PETALS —
Cherokee Rose

STEM AND
FLOWER CENTER —
Clover

SMALL LEAF —
Honey Comb

LARGE LEAF — Bluebell

Floorcloth Stencils (continued)

STENCIL C

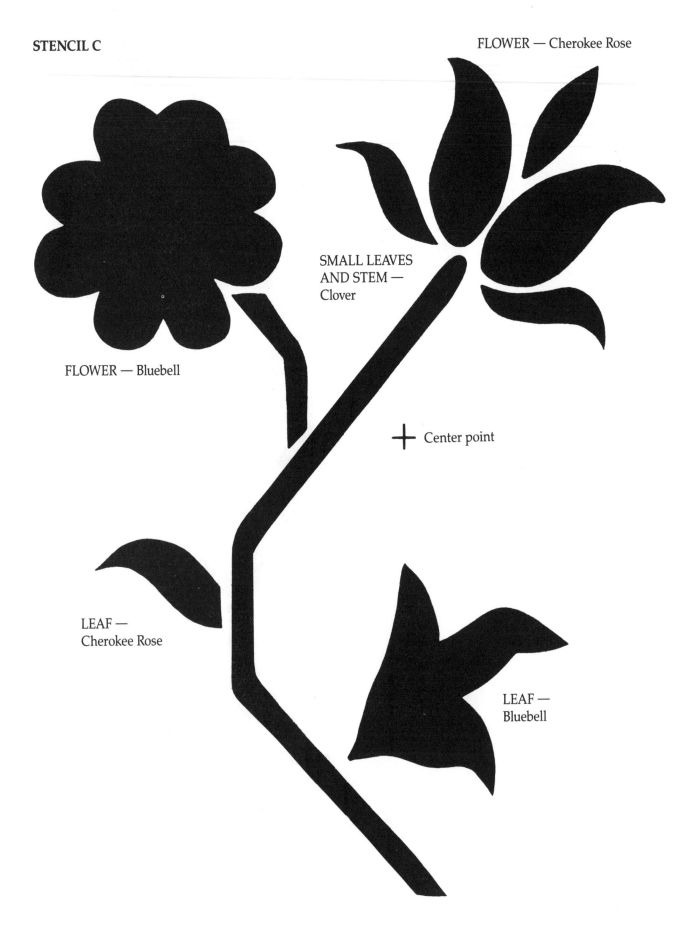

FLOWER — Cherokee Rose

SMALL LEAVES AND STEM — Clover

FLOWER — Bluebell

+ Center point

LEAF — Cherokee Rose

LEAF — Bluebell

Floorcloth Stencils (continued)

STENCIL D

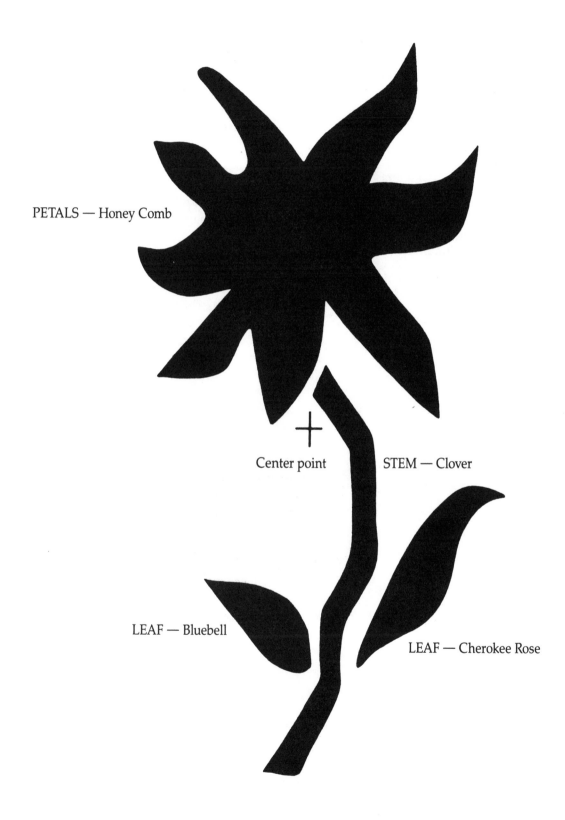

PETALS — Honey Comb

Center point

STEM — Clover

LEAF — Bluebell

LEAF — Cherokee Rose

Painted Welcome Board

THIS project demonstrates how stencils can be used to simulate the look of a charming, Grandma Moses–style painting. In making this board, you will be introduced to another method of stenciling — sponge painting (with a natural cosmetic sponge). This bucolic board will look wonderful displayed on a shelf, over your door, or on the mantel as a heartwarming greeting to all who come to call. If you prefer a painting, stencil the design on ¼" plywood (sanded and sealed), omit the "Welcome," and frame it. Either way, be prepared for a beautiful addition to your home and the accolades of your friends. You can turn your board into a versatile year-round accessory by stenciling a wintry version, complete with a Christmas greeting, on the reverse side.

Feel free to place the animals, people, trees, and so forth wherever you like in the design. There is no need to follow my suggestions if you have an idea that you prefer.

SUPPLIES

10" x 22" sheet of tracing paper, pencil
2' length of 1" x 10" pine
Saber or band saw
Sandpaper (medium and fine)
Tack cloth
Wood sealer, brush
Graphite paper
14" x 18" sheet of Mylar, X-acto knife, pane of glass, masking tape
Acrylic paint (Folk Art colors: black, Red Clay, white, Buttercup, Bluebell, Clover, Coffee Bean, Thicket, Honey Comb, Patchwork Green, Nutmeg)
Extender
1" sponge brush, No. 4 natural-bristle bright brush, No. 0 round brush, small stencil brushes
Paper plate, paper towels
Natural cosmetic (sea) sponge
Water-based varnish (optional)

PREPARATION

1. Fold the sheet of tracing paper in half and place the half pattern on the fold, as indicated on the pattern (page 82). Trace the pattern and the horizon lines onto the paper. Keep the paper folded in half as you cut out the half pattern, making a full-size pattern when the paper is unfolded. Trace the pattern (outline only) onto the wood and cut it out with a saber saw or band saw. Sand, wipe with a tack cloth, and seal (see Chapter 1, page 19).

2. With the 1" sponge brush, paint the side edges and the back of the board with Red Clay. Remove any paint that runs to the front.

3. Use the graphite paper to transfer the horizon lines to the board (draw the pond on one side only).

4. With the exception of the house, which will be cut as a three-part color-separated stencil, all the designs (pages 83–84) are full-design stencils. Remember to leave a 1" margin around each. Refer to the instructions at the beginning of the chapter (page 68), if necessary.

PAINTING AND STENCILING

1. To create the sky, place some Bluebell and some white paint separately on a paper plate. Thin the Bluebell with water to the consistency of milk. Dip the 1" sponge brush into the Bluebell and, starting at the top of the board, paint the upper half of the sky, moving from left to right. Blot the brush on a paper towel, dip it into the white paint, and, starting at the horizon line, paint the remaining half of the sky, blending the colors together in the middle (the sky should be light blue). Paint the pond with this Bluebell/white blend.

The clouds will be sponge-painted. (Practice this technique on a piece of scrap paper before going to your board. See Figure 4-8.) Dip a

FIG. 4-8. *Practicing sponge stenciling.*

corner of the cosmetic sponge in the white paint (don't add water), blot it lightly on a paper towel, then gently dab the sponge on the sky for clouds, leaving the centers free of paint for a fluffier look.

2. Place some Patchwork Green and some Buttercup on a paper plate. Thin each slightly with water so they will spread easily. Dip a sponge brush into the green and, moving from left to right, paint two thirds of the center ground area from the horizon line down. Blot the brush on a paper towel to remove most of the green, dip it in Buttercup, and paint from the bottom edge up, blending the colors together (keeping the green toward the top and the Buttercup toward the bottom) until there is no visible line of demarcation. Use the bright brush to paint the hills on the right, one Clover and the other Honey Comb. On the left, paint one hill Nutmeg and the other Honey Comb.

3. Center house stencil A and stencil it with white. (You will have to build up several layers to cover the background colors completely.) Remove stencil A, align stencil B, and stencil the windows and roof with black. Replace stencil B with C and complete the house by stenciling the shutters and chimneys with Red Clay.

4. Try the natural bright brush for stenciling the small areas, and then switch to a round brush to paint the details. Stencil a white fence in the lower right corner. Thin the paint (white or Nutmeg) with extender and use a No. 0 round brush to paint a small fence along the edge of the hills.

5. Stencil a large tree trunk on each side of the board with Coffee Bean; if desired, stencil smaller trees along the horizon line. To create the appearance of trees growing from the ground, fade the color as you get toward the bottom of the trunks. Before removing the stencils, lightly shade one edge of each with black. Sponge-paint foliage on the branches with Clover, shade with Thicket, and highlight with Buttercup. (For a fall scene, sponge with Red Clay and Buttercup instead.)

6. Position the narrow end of the path stencil at the bottom of the door and stencil along the edges with Honey Comb (allow some of the ground to show through). With the tip of the sponge dipped in Clover and Thicket, sponge a small hedge flanking the path and small bushes in front of the house.

7. Stencil the animals and people. Paint the details — shoes, hair bow, apron, bells on sheep, spots on the dog — with a round brush. So that the figures appear to be grounded rather than floating in midair, dry-brush a little Honey Comb under each.

8. Center the "WELCOME" stencil ½" from the top edge of the board (the letter C should be at the exact center), tape it in place, and stencil it with black paint.

9. Small details such as multicolored flowers along the paths, apples in the trees, and cabbages or pumpkins in the garden can be added by dipping the wooden end of your round brush or a stylus in paint and dotting where needed. Add texture to the grassy areas by sponging them lightly with Clover. If you feel comfortable with freehand painting, hang a swing from the tree or place birds in a nest, panes in the windows, or morning glories trailing along the fence. When the paint has thoroughly dried, finish the project with one or two coats of satin-finish water-based varnish, if desired.

Detail from color plate 8.

Welcome Board
Half Pattern

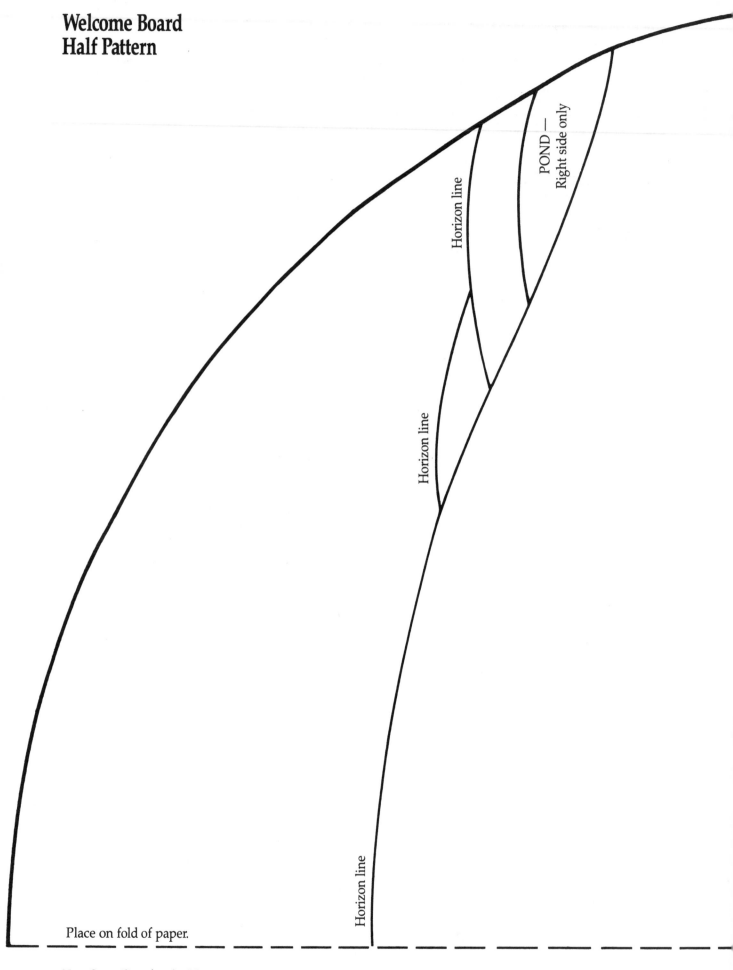

Horizon line

POND —
Right side only

Horizon line

Horizon line

Place on fold of paper.

Welcome Board Stencils

HOUSE STENCIL A — White

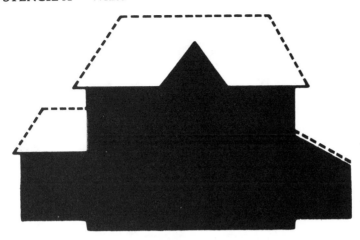

HOUSE STENCIL B
ROOF, WINDOWS — Black

HOUSE STENCIL C
SHUTTERS, CHIMNEYS, DOOR
— Red Clay

Welcome Board
Stencils (continued)

ANIMALS

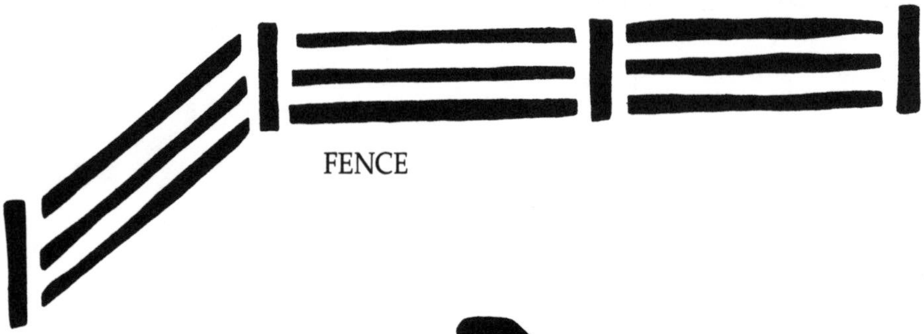

FENCE

PATH

PEOPLE

TREES

5
Toys for the Young at Heart

TWENTIETH-CENTURY children have been brought up with elaborate mechanical toys, toys that speak, walk, and perform just about every human function imaginable. Fascinating as they may be, somehow they rob the child of the opportunity to stretch his or her imagination. Toys from the past were less sophisticated, often crudely made. They had all the essential elements of what they were supposed to be but few unnecessary details; all they lacked was a child's imagination to bring them to life.

Many of these early toys were patterned after commonly seen and used items, and because farming was such a common occupation in nineteenth-century America, barnyard animals and farm implements were often the inspiration for toy makers. With woolly sheep, carved horses on wheeled platforms, and small wagons, children could, on a small scale, imitate their farmer parents. Dolls were fashioned from whatever materials could be found — dried apples, cornhusks, scraps of wood and fabric, even feed sacks. Their homespun, whimsical qualities, fashioned with loving hands, are what endear them to collectors, perhaps evoking memories of the collector's own childhood.

Many people are fortunate enough to have relatives who squirreled away some of these treasures for future generations, but for the rest of us, some of the same joys of childhood can be rekindled in the making and giving of the delightful country-style toys in this chapter. No matter how old we are, making special toys for the children in our lives can make us feel young at heart. (I always feel a bit like one of Santa's elves.) An often unanticipated bonus is the lasting impression such a toy can make on the recipient. While playing recently with a favorite pull toy, my five-year-old daughter asked, "Mom, do you remember when you sat in that chair and made this sheep for me?" That's the kind of memory that can't be bought!

Sheep Pull Toy

ONE of the most popular nineteenth-century toys was the woolly sheep, then covered with real lamb's wool. Its appeal is timeless. This version, either on a wheeled platform or freestanding, will make a perfect gift for a new baby, your favorite child, or yourself.

SUPPLIES

Tracing and graphite paper, pencil
2″ x 6″ x 7″ piece of pine
Band or saber saw
Carving knife (optional)
Medium-grit sandpaper
Four 4″ round wooden clothespins
Eight ⅝″ wire nails and eight 1″ black paneling nails, hammer, pliers
Black acrylic paint, 1-ounce bottle
1″ sponge brush
10″ x 14″ piece of off-white fleece fabric
10″ x 12″ piece of polyester batting
2″ square of black felt
Needle and white thread, scissors, straight pins
Two handfuls of polyester fiber stuffing
Quick-drying glue
½ yard of ¼″ ribbon, ½″ bell with a loop for a ribbon
½″ x 6″ x 7″ piece of pine
Rust or blue acrylic paint, 1-ounce bottle (optional)
Drill with 1/16″ and 3/16″ bits
3′ of sisal twine, small bead for the end
Four 2″ cast-metal wheels (see Source Guide on page 159)
Four No. 6 flat washers

Detail from color plate 1.

MAKING THE SHEEP'S BODY

1. Trace body pattern A on tracing paper and transfer the pattern with graphite paper to the 2″-thick block of pine. Cut out the pattern with a band or saber saw. Since the head of a sheep is much narrower than the body, trim the neck and head area (Figure 5-1) to a thickness of 1″ by removing ½″ from each side with a carving knife or band saw. Sand the head section to smooth and round the edges.

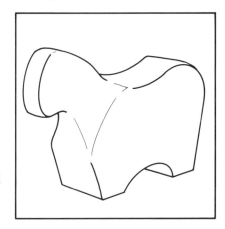

FIG. 5-1. *Trim the neck and head area.*

2. Saw the lower half off one side of each clothespin to make the legs. (See Figure 5-2.) It's important that the legs are all the same length, so be certain that you saw at exactly the same point on each one.

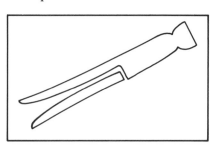

FIG. 5-2. *Remove half of one side of the clothespins.*

3. The legs will be attached to the body using wire nails. Since the clothespins are made of hardwood and have a tendency to split when nailed, it helps to blunt the tip of each nail before proceeding. To do this, hold the nail with pliers so that the head is resting against a hard base (such as a concrete floor) and strike the point of the nail with a hammer. Position the first two legs vertically on the body block, as shown in Figure 5-3, and attach them with two nails through each. Nail one of the remaining two legs to the other side of the body. (If you want the sheep to appear to be walking rather than standing, stagger the legs slightly.) Turn the sheep right side up and position the remaining leg so that all "hooves" rest evenly on a flat surface. Adjust as necessary and nail. If you're making a free-standing sheep, the position of the legs is not as critical.

(Text continues on page 89.)

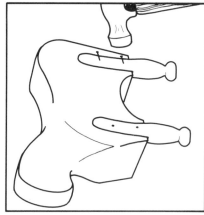

FIG. 5-3. *Attaching the legs to the sheep body.*

Sheep Pull Toy
Wood Patterns

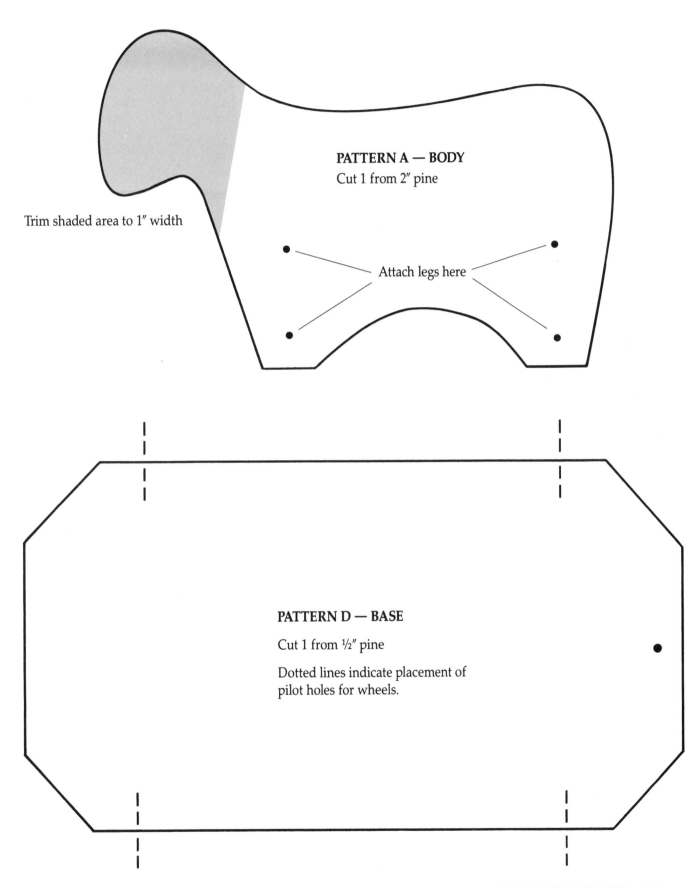

Trim shaded area to 1″ width

PATTERN A — BODY

Cut 1 from 2″ pine

Attach legs here

PATTERN D — BASE

Cut 1 from ½″ pine

Dotted lines indicate placement of pilot holes for wheels.

Sheep Pull Toy
Fabric Patterns

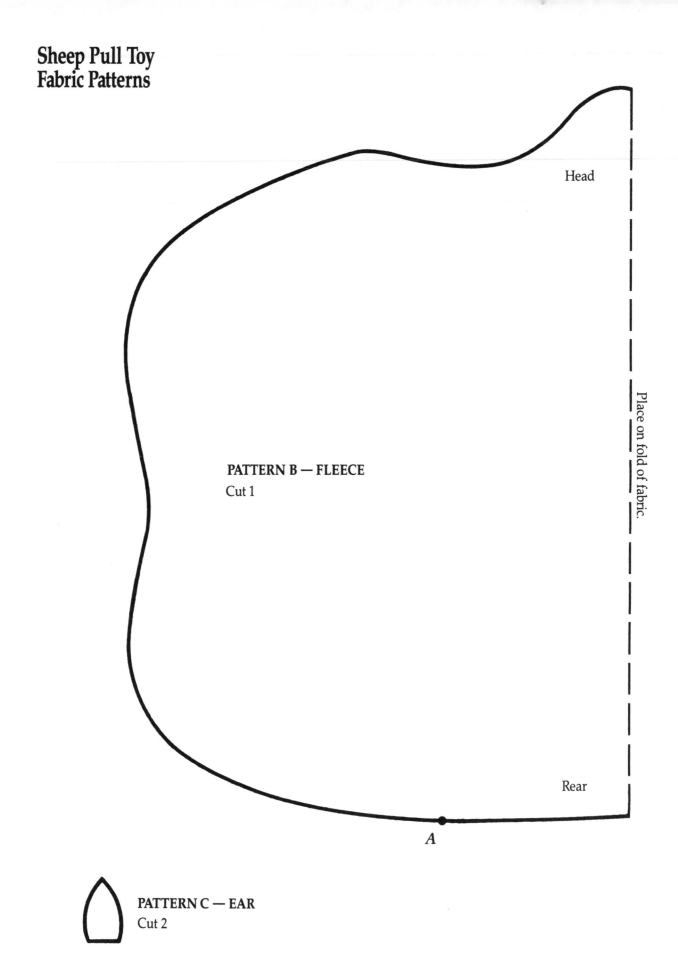

Head

Place on fold of fabric.

PATTERN B — FLEECE
Cut 1

Rear

A

PATTERN C — EAR
Cut 2

4. Paint the legs, neck, and head black. Let the paint dry.

5. Make a tracing-paper pattern from pattern B. Fold the fleece fabric in half wrong side out, pin the pattern to the wrong side of the fleece, and cut. Cut a piece of batting ¼" smaller than the fleece. Cut two ears from black felt using pattern C.

6. Place the batting on the wrong side of the fleece and center the sheep's body on both (Figure 5-4). Wrap both pieces around the body (the fleece will be very loose but will fill out when stuffed), bringing the edges together on the underside of the sheep to make a seam. Hold with straight pins. Sew the fleece together securely from the front legs to the rear legs (Figure 5-5). Bring the fleece together between the front

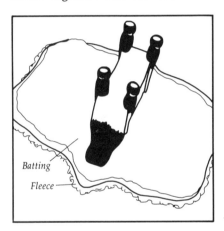

FIG. 5-4. *Center the sheep body on the fleece and batting.*

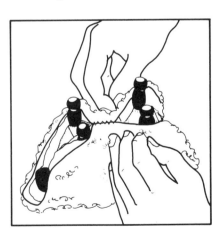

FIG. 5-5. *Sew the fleece together between the legs.*

legs and sew; bring it together between the rear legs and sew, pulling the fleece as close to the legs as possible (Figure 5-6). Leave the ends open for stuffing. Working from both ends, lightly stuff the body (between the batting and the wood block) with the polyester stuffing. (It's designed to be quite stocky.)

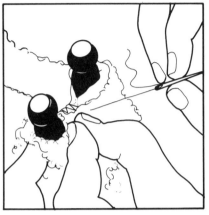

FIG. 5-6. *Sew the fleece tightly around each leg.*

7. The excess fabric on the top rear end of the sheep will be used to form a U-shaped tail. Sew the fleece together from the rear legs up, stopping 2" from the top. Starting at point A (Figure 5-7), sew with a long, loose running stitch through one layer only, 1" from the edge of the fleece, all around the opening (from

FIG. 5-7. *Sew around the opening, beginning and ending at point A.*

A back to A). Pull the thread tight, gathering the fleece into a tail (Figure 5-8). Tie a knot in the end of the thread to secure it. Tack the tip of the tail down to the rump area (so it isn't sticking straight up) with a few tiny stitches (Figure 5-9).

FIG. 5-8. *Pull the thread tight to form a tail.*

FIG. 5-9. *Tack the tail down to the rump.*

8. Continue to stuff and shape the body through the front opening. When you are satisfied with the shape, sew the opening closed, stopping under the chin. Once again, sew a loose running stitch around the opening, this time keeping your stitch as close to the edge of the fleece as possible. Pull the thread to gather the fleece snugly around the face, then knot the end of the thread to secure it. (See Figure 5-10.) If necessary, trim and glue the edge of the fleece around the face. Position the ears close to the edge of the fabric and stitch them in place. Tie the ribbon and bell around the neck. If you don't want a pull toy, the sheep may be considered complete at this point.

FIG. 5-10. *Gather the fleece around the face.*

MAKING THE PLATFORM

1. Trace pattern D (page 87) onto the ½" pine, cut it out with a band or saber saw, and sand it. For an antique look, paint the edges black and the top and bottom rust or blue, let the paint dry, and antique. (See Chapter 1, page 20, for antiquing techniques.)

2. Drill a ³⁄₁₆" hole in the center of one end of the platform and thread the twine through the hole. Knot the twine underneath to secure it and put a bead on the pull end, kept in place with knots before and after it.

3. To facilitate the attachment of the wheels, use a ¹⁄₁₆" bit to drill four pilot holes in the sides of the platform, about ⅝" deep. The holes should be spaced 1¼" from each end (see pattern D) and centered between the top and bottom *on the sides* of the platform.

4. (NOTE: Antique the metal wheels before you attach them; see Chapter 1, page 21.) Place a washer between each wheel and the platform, then using the pilot holes as guides, nail two wheels to one side of the platform. Leave enough space between the head of the nail and the wheel to allow it to rotate freely. Turn the platform over. To prevent the wheels on the first side from being pushed into the platform while you are hammering on the second set of wheels, place a small piece of scrap wood between the wheels to elevate the platform from the surface of your worktable. With the platform resting on the block of wood, attach the remaining wheels.

5. Position the sheep on the platform. Lift the right legs off the platform slightly and mark the platform where the center of the legs will rest. Repeat for the left legs. Using a ¹⁄₁₆" bit, drill four pilot holes through the platform at the points where the legs will be attached. Place the sheep on its back, legs up. Place the platform upside down on the "hooves" and attach the sheep to the platform by driving a paneling nail through each pilot hole into a leg. Hold each leg firmly in place to prevent it from being loosened from the body while you drive in the nail. When all four legs are attached, turn the sheep right side up and make sure that it is securely fastened to the platform.

Chunky Blocks

IF YOU can persuade your budding builder to share these blocks, you can use them as clever decorative accents in some unexpected places. In groups of three, they make wonderful bookends; or make enough to spell your child's name or a homespun "Welcome" that can't be missed. But don't be surprised when your greeting once again turns into a child's house of blocks!

SUPPLIES
4″ x 4″ x 12″ piece of cedar (makes three blocks)
Square
Crosscut handsaw
Rasp or plane
Sandpaper (medium and fine)
Tack cloth
Acrylic paint
Stain (optional)
1″ sponge brush (for the base coat)
9″ x 13″ sheet of Mylar, X-acto knife, pane of glass, pencil, masking tape
Several small stencil brushes

MAKING THE BLOCKS

1. Measure 3½″ from a squared end of the wood and mark; with a square, extend this mark completely around the block. Use this line as a cutting guide and saw through the wood. Repeat twice. Round the edges and corners of the three blocks with a rasp or plane. Use an electric sander or hand-sand to smooth all sides, beginning with medium-grit paper and finishing with fine. Wipe with a tack cloth.

2. Paint or stain the wood. If you decide to paint the blocks, basecoat them with a light color (ivory or beige).

3. Cut the Mylar into six 3½″ squares. Choose your stencil patterns (three letters and three pictures for each block), trace, and cut. (Stencil patterns continue on pages 92–94.)

4. Stencil the letters on the blocks — one on the top, one on the side, and one on the bottom. Then stencil the border design in a contrasting color around each letter (blue or black letters, red border).

5. Stencil a picture design on the remaining three sides.

6. These blocks look best with a well-worn finish, so I suggest antiquing them using the instructions in Chapter 1 (page 20).

Detail from color plate 2.

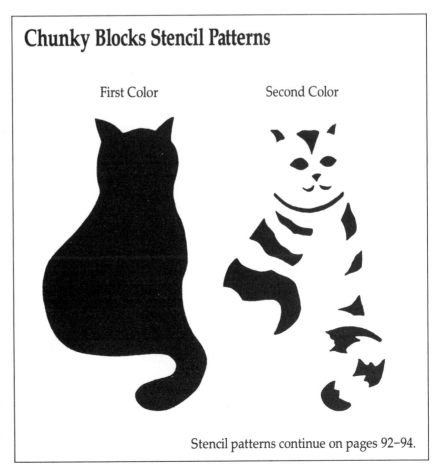

Chunky Blocks Stencil Patterns

First Color   Second Color

Stencil patterns continue on pages 92–94.

A B C D

E F G H

I J K L

M N O P

Q R S T

Chunky Blocks Stencil Patterns (continued)

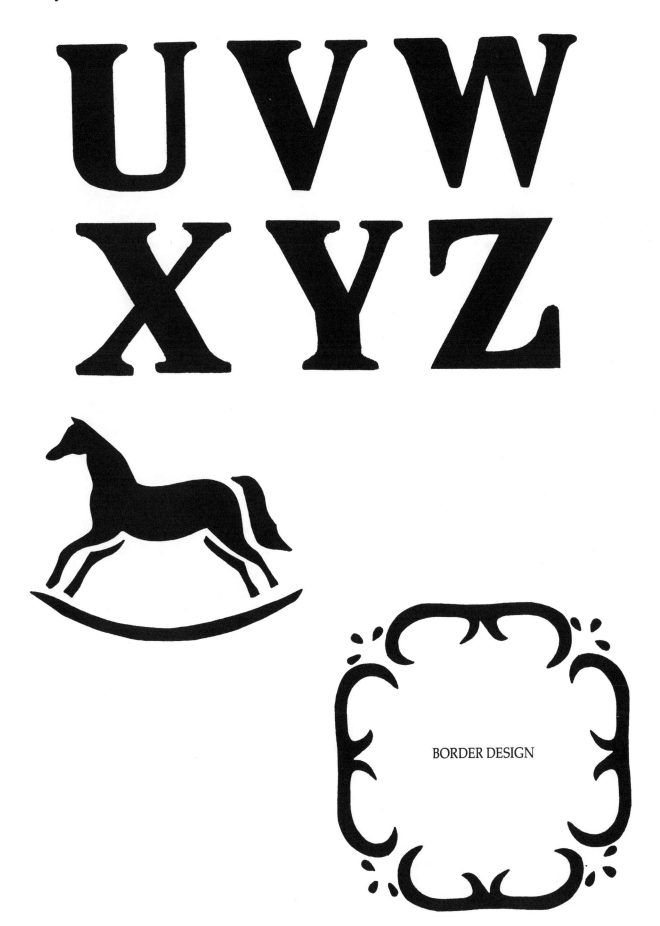

BORDER DESIGN

Chunky Blocks Stencil Patterns (continued)

First Color   Second Color

First Color   Second Color

Captivating Kittens

THESE adorable kittens are guaranteed to bring a smile when your child discovers that, with a turn of the kitten's head, its tail moves as well! (The head and tail are attached to a dowel that runs through the body.) This pint-size toy (5" tall from paw to tail) captures the spirit and whimsy of folk art and is easy to make. Follow the color suggestions below or surprise your little ones with a likeness of their very own feline.

SUPPLIES
3" length of 2" x 3" pine
2"-square piece of 1" pine
¼" x ⅞" x 4" piece of pine
2¼" length of ¼" dowel
Band or saber saw
Tracing and graphite paper, pencil, tape, scissors
Sandpaper (medium and fine)
Drill with ¼" and 17/64" bits
Tacky glue
No. 1 round, No. 1 and No. 4 flat bristle brushes
Paper plate, paper towels
Acrylic paint (suggested colors: black, brown, white, gold, pink)
Extender
12" piece of ⅛" or ¼" ribbon

Detail from color plate 9.

CUTTING THE PIECES

NOTE: If you plan to use a saber saw for this project, you will need to use larger pieces of wood than those specified in the supply list (double the length for each). The extra wood is needed to clamp each piece to your worktable while you are cutting (use a 4" C-clamp). In addition, you will have to make the cuts from each side of the piece, ending at the point closest to the clamp because the saw will not be able to rotate in a full circle.

1. Rip cut (cut with the grain) the 2" x 3" pine to a width of 1⅝". With the cut side down, trace pattern A (page 96 — side view) to the piece, aligning it so that the feet are at one end. Remove the wood between the legs. Turn the piece on its side and trace pattern B (front view), legs aligned from the same end. Cut and sand. Drill a 17/64" hole all the way through the body at the point marked on pattern B.

2. Using graphite paper, transfer pattern C to the 1" pine, with the ears at one end. Drill a ¼" hole to a depth of approximately ½" at the point marked on the pattern. Cut and sand.

3. Using graphite paper, transfer pattern D to the ¼" pine, with the tail parallel to the grain of the wood. Drill a ¼" hole through the tail at the point marked on the pattern. Cut and sand.

4. Sand the 2¼" length of ¼" dowel. Apply glue to the hole in the tail and insert the dowel into the hole until it is flush on the other side.

PAINTING THE KITTEN

Use a No. 1 round brush for the detail painting and the flat brushes for all other painting.

1. Basecoat the head, tail, body, and dowel black (or color of your choice). Let the paint dry.

2. Since it is important that the face pattern be aligned perfectly on the head, one extra step is used in the transferring process to ensure this. Trace the face pattern onto a small piece of tracing paper and coat the reverse side with pencil lead. Cut out around the outline of the head. Align this cut-out pattern on the head, pencil side down, hold it in place, and trace all markings and features.

3. Use a No. 1 flat bristle brush and the dry-brush technique to paint the white areas on the face. (Refer to the face painting guide, page 96.) Dip the brush in white paint and then stroke it on a paper towel until the brush is *almost dry*. Carefully paint the areas surrounding the eyes, the muzzle, and the chin using short, light, outward strokes. Dry-brush white areas of fur onto the chest, paws, and tail if desired (add patches of gold for a calico cat).

4. Paint the eyes gold, with black pupils. Highlight each pupil with a tiny fleck of white.

5. Blend a small amount of brown and pink and paint the nose. Dry-brush some of this mixture inside each ear. Highlight the tip of the nose with a tiny fleck of white.

6. Thin a small amount of black paint with extender and lightly outline the mouth, nose, and eyes to define them. Add black and white whiskers.

(Text continues on next page.)

PUTTING IT TOGETHER

1. Insert the dowel through the body. Put a small amount of glue in the hole in the head. Holding the tail, gently push the head onto the dowel. Tail and head should move together freely, and they should stay in any position you put them.

2. Tie the ribbon into a bow around the neck.

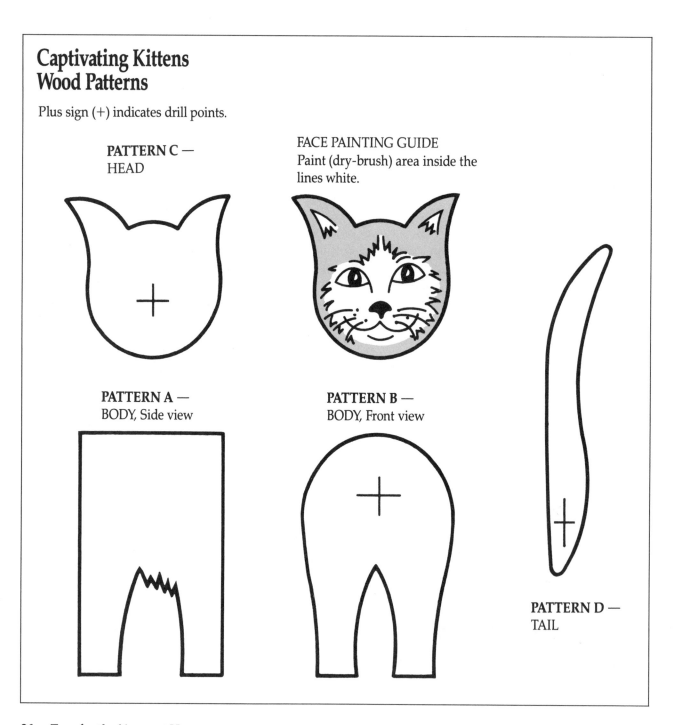

Captivating Kittens
Wood Patterns

Plus sign (+) indicates drill points.

PATTERN C —
HEAD

FACE PAINTING GUIDE
Paint (dry-brush) area inside the lines white.

PATTERN A —
BODY, Side view

PATTERN B —
BODY, Front view

PATTERN D —
TAIL

Wooden Folk Dolls

THESE charming hand-painted dolls are an updated version of wooden dolls so popular many years ago. Their carefully painted faces and jointed movable legs lend them such individual appeal and personality that they are certain to claim a special place in any doll lover's heart. Although they might look difficult to paint, you'll be surprised at how easy they are to do. Surprise a doll collector or a special child with one or both of these country kids!

SUPPLIES

Two 1" x 6" x 10" pieces of pine (for two dolls)
Tracing and graphite paper, pencil, tape, scissors
Band or saber saw
Drill with ⅛" and ⁵⁄₆₄" bits
Two 8d finishing nails for pattern A, two 4d finishing nails for pattern B
Hammer
Acrylic paint (Folk Art colors: Skintone, white, Bluebell, Slate Blue, black, Coffee Bean, Red Clay, Rusty Nail, Honey Comb, Taffy)
Extender
No. 1 round, No. 4 and No. 6 flat brushes
Paper plate, paper towels
Stylus or toothpick
24" length of ¼" three-ply manila rope
20" piece of ⅛" red satin ribbon for pattern A
Hot-glue gun or tacky glue and an old brush for spreading
Two 3½" to 4" straw hats (available at craft shops)
Fine sandpaper or steel wool for antiquing (optional)
Wood sealer and 1" sponge brush

Detail from color plate 1.

PREPARATION

1. Using graphite paper, transfer the body pattern outline and the drill guidelines (A=Amanda, page 98; B=John, page 100) to one end of the 1" pine. Lay the pattern out carefully — you will have just enough wood to cut the body and two legs from one piece. Cut with a band or saber saw. Make sure the slots for the legs are cut accurately (the legs will not move freely if, for example, the slots are crooked or too small). Transfer the leg pattern to the other end of the pine, with the back of the leg aligned on an edge; cut it out. Repeat for the other leg. Sand and seal all pieces; let them dry.

2. Since the accurate alignment of the leg pivot holes through the doll is critical to the proper movement of the legs, you must mark where the drill will enter and leave the wood. Extend the drill guideline from the front around the outside of the doll and through the inside of the leg slots. Mark the midpoint of this line on each side of the doll and on the inside of each leg slot. Use the midpoint marks as guides and, with the doll resting on its side, drill with a ⅛" bit for pattern A or a ⁵⁄₆₄" bit for pattern B (Figure 5-11). *Do not* drill into the center piece of wood between the leg slots.

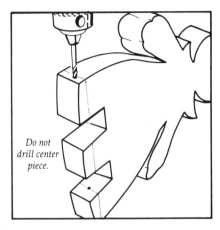

Do not drill center piece.

FIG. 5-11. *Drilling the holes for the leg pivots.*

3. With the doll on its back, insert a leg in a slot. Gently tap a nail (8d for Amanda, 4d for John) through the hole into the leg just far enough to allow leg movement without the nail falling out. Check the movement of the leg. Reposition the nail if necessary to allow the leg to pivot to a sitting position. (See Figure 5-12.) When you are satisfied, remove the leg and drill a hole through it where the nail was. Reinsert the leg in the slot and drive the nail flush. Repeat for the other side.

(Text continues on page 99.)

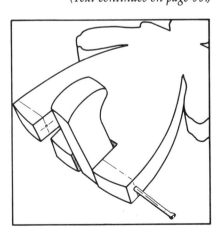

FIG. 5-12. *Insert a nail and test the leg movement.*

Wooden Folk Doll
Pattern A — Amanda

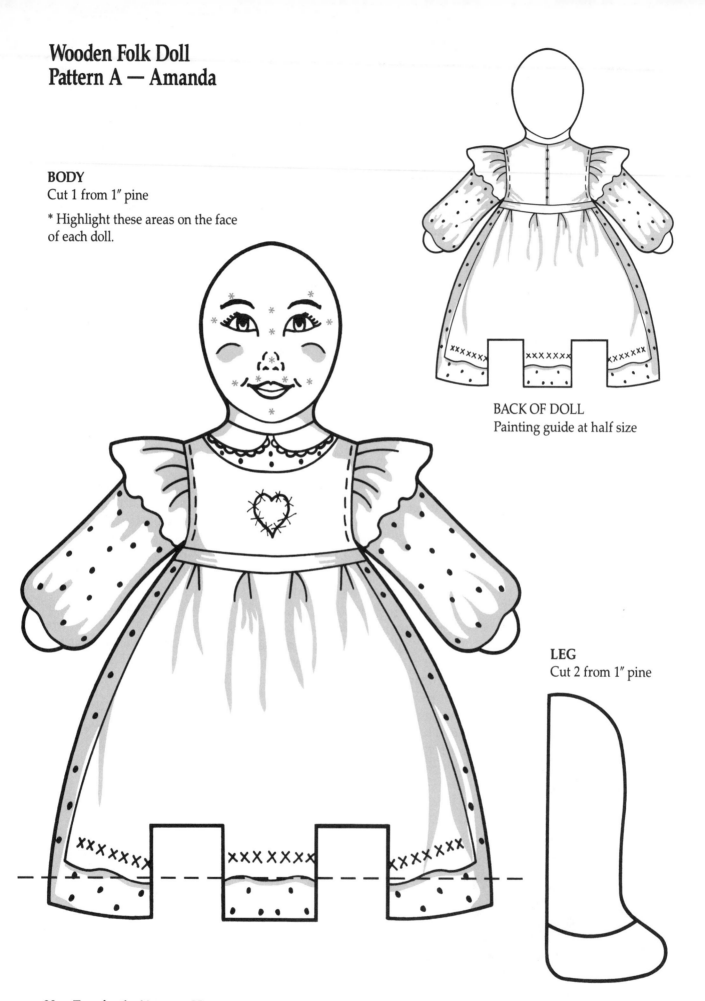

BODY

Cut 1 from 1″ pine

* Highlight these areas on the face
of each doll.

BACK OF DOLL
Painting guide at half size

LEG
Cut 2 from 1″ pine

PAINTING THE FACES

Follow steps 1–7 for painting both dolls' faces. (See the pattern.) For all detail painting, use a No. 1 round brush with very little paint on it. When a thinned color is called for, dip the tip of your brush into extender, then into the paint (the paint will flow more smoothly, producing a finer line). When a blended color is called for, place a small amount of each color on a paper plate (an amount about the size of a pencil eraser) and mix it thoroughly before loading your brush.

1. Basecoat the head, face, neck, and both hands with Skintone. It might take two or three coats to cover the wood completely. Trace the head outline and facial features (from the body pattern) on a small piece of tracing paper. Coat the reverse side of the paper with pencil lead and cut out the pattern along the head outline. Then position the pattern on the doll and lightly retrace the facial features.

2. Paint the white areas of the eyes (see Figure 5-13), then paint the irises Bluebell. While the paint is wet, paint the upper half of each eye Slate Blue and blend the colors. This will add depth to the irises. Paint the pu-pils black and highlight each with a tiny fleck of white. Blend Skintone and Coffee Bean on your palette and use it to paint the lashes and brows and to outline the eyes lightly. Add a few tiny black lashes.

3. Outline the nose with thinned Coffee Bean.

4. Blend Red Clay and Skintone (the color should be quite pale) and paint the mouth. Define the mouth by outlining the lip and smile lines with thinned Coffee Bean. Highlight the bottom lip with a fleck of white.

5. Blend Skintone, Rusty Nail, and extender to get a medium-pink color; then using a flat brush, dry-brush (see Glossary, page 157) a half-moon–shaped blush on each cheek (refer to the pattern), blending to eliminate all demarcation lines. If desired, add Skintone–Coffee Bean freckles.

6. Define the neckline by painting the neck with Skintone and Honey Comb. Outline the jawline with thinned Coffee Bean.

7. Highlight the areas of the face indicated on the pattern by asterisks by dry-brushing with a blend of Skintone, Taffy, and extender.

PAINTING THE CLOTHES

At this point, the similarity between the boy and girl dolls ends. Use graphite paper to transfer or draw freehand the clothing pattern to the front and back of the doll. When shading is called for (indicated by shaded areas on the pattern), paint on the still-wet base coat. Blend the base color and extender on a flat brush, dip the edge of the brush into the darker color, then blend the paint into your brush before painting by stroking it on your palette a few times. If the color becomes too dark, repeat the previous steps with the base color until you get the desired results.

Amanda: Thin Bluebell with water and basecoat the dress; shade it with Slate Blue. With a stylus or toothpick, paint small white dots on the dress. Paint the collar white with white lace trim. Basecoat the pinafore Taffy; for a ruffled look, shade it with Honey Comb. Outline the seam lines at the waist and shoulder with Honey Comb. Lightly trace or draw the heart on the pinafore. Paint a series of tiny Xs (to resemble a cross-stitch) around the edge of the heart and along the bottom of the pinafore with Red Clay. With thinned Red Clay, trim the edge of the sleeve ruffles, paint the buttons on the back, and paint the topstitching. Paint the legs below the dress Taffy and the shoes black.

John: Basecoat the shirt Taffy and shade it with Honey Comb; outline the collar and shirt at the wrists with thinned Honey Comb. Paint stripes on the shirt with thinned Red Clay. Paint buttons with a stylus or the wooden end of your brush dipped in white. Basecoat the knickers and suspenders Honey Comb and shade with Coffee Bean. Outline the suspenders, pockets, and waistband with thinned Coffee Bean. Paint the buttons white. Paint the feet and legs below the knickers Skintone.

(Text continues on page 101.)

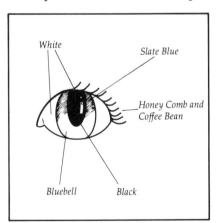

FIG. 5-13. *Color guide for the eyes.*

Wooden Folk Doll
Pattern B — John

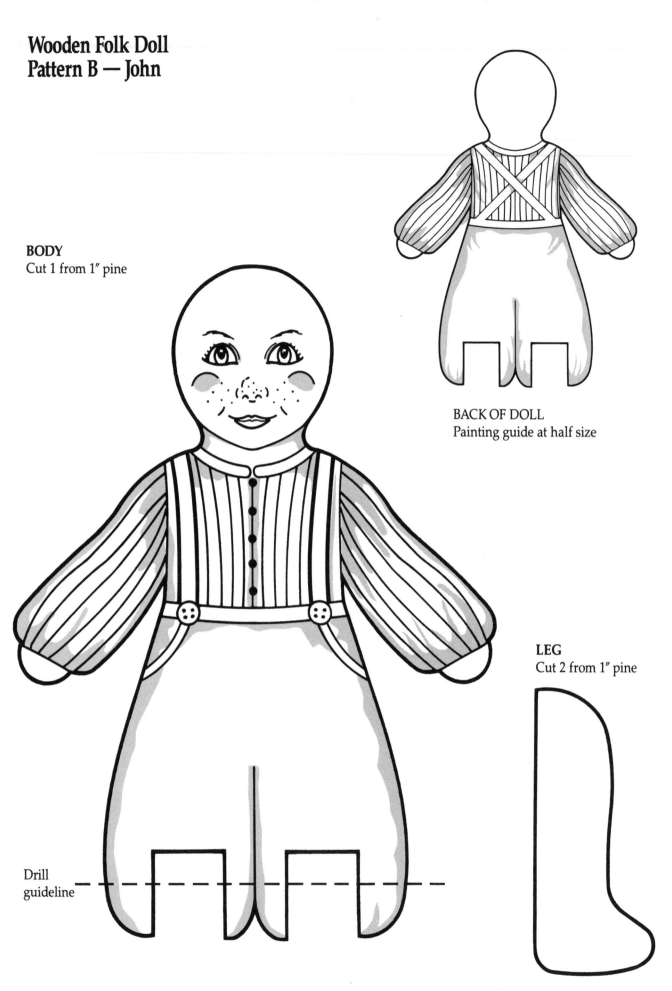

BODY
Cut 1 from 1″ pine

BACK OF DOLL
Painting guide at half size

LEG
Cut 2 from 1″ pine

Drill
guideline

ATTACHING THE HAIR

Since the hat will be covering the back of the head, it is not necessary to attach hair to that part of the head.

Amanda: If bangs are desired, unravel and fray a 1½″ length of manila rope and glue it to the top and forehead of the doll before attaching the braids (Figure 5-14). Cut two 4″ lengths of rope for braids. Hold one end tightly and unravel and straighten 1½″ at the other end. Spread glue ⅛″ around the edge of the face, on the side and top of the head. Press and hold the straightened hair in place on one side until the glue is dry. Repeat on the other side. (See Figure 5-15.) Fray the lower ½″ of the braids and add small bows. Generously spread glue on the top and back of the head; then press and hold the hat in place until the glue is dry (about one minute). Add a ribbon and bow to the hat if desired.

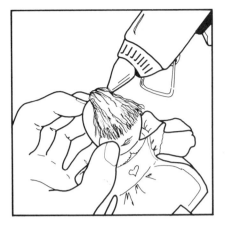

FIG. 5-14. *Attaching the bangs with a glue gun.*

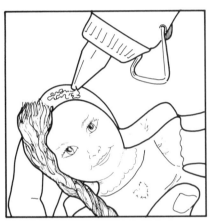

FIG. 5-15. *Attaching the braids.*

John: Cut three 1½″ lengths of rope. Separate each into three thin strands. While holding one end tightly, unravel and straighten all but the very end of each. Spread glue across the forehead and on top of the head; press and hold the bangs in place until the glue is dry. Spread glue along the edge of the face and the side of the head and continue to layer short, frayed sections of hair around the face. Trim the hair if necessary to get a bowl-type haircut. Glue the hat in place.

ANTIQUING

If you want the dolls to have a well-loved, played-with look, lightly sand and round the edges with fine sandpaper or steel wool.

Express Wagon

GENERATIONS ago nearly every child wished for and, if lucky, treasured a little red wagon. This miniature reproduction of an early Victorian coaster wagon is both decorative and fun to play with. It makes a delightful gift for a special child, or you can fill it with a collection of folk dolls or teddies for the perfect finishing touch in your country home. Since this project has many parts, it requires a little more time than the others in this chapter, but I'm sure you'll agree that the results are well worth the effort.

SUPPLIES

24" length of ¼" x 2⅝" clear pine lattice

17" length of ¼" x 1⅜" clear pine lattice

24" length of ¼" x 1⅝" clear pine lattice

16" length of ½" x 2½" pine

9" length of ¼" dowel and 1" length of ⅜" dowel

Scroll or band saw

Sandpaper (medium and fine)

Wood glue

Eighteen ½", two ¾", and one 1¼" brads, hammer

Long-nose pliers (with wire-cutter feature)

Drill with ¹⁄₁₆", ⁵⁄₆₄", ⁵⁄₃₂", ¼", and No. 8 counterbore bits

Acrylic paint (Folk Art colors: Red Clay, black, Harvest Gold)

1" sponge brush, No. 1 round brush, two small stencil brushes

Extender

One 6d finishing nail, four 1" black paneling nails

Ruler

Tracing and graphite paper

2" x 11" sheet of Mylar, pencil, X-acto knife, pane of glass, masking tape, black felt-tip marker (optional)

One 1¼" No. 6 flat-head wood screw, screwdriver

Six No. 6 flat washers

Four 2" cast-metal wheels (see the Source Guide on page 159)

CONSTRUCTING THE BOX
(Refer to Figure 5-17)

1. Whenever possible, place the straight side of a pattern along the planed edge of the wood to obtain the most efficient and economical use of the wood. For the bottom (A), cut and sand two 11" pieces from the 2⅝" lattice; for the end panels (B), cut and sand two 5¼" pieces from the 1⅜" lattice; and for the side panels (C), cut and sand two 11" pieces from the 1⅝" lattice.

2. Place the two bottom pieces side by side on a flat surface. Apply glue evenly to the bottom edge of one end panel and carefully position it on one end of the box bottom; all the edges should be flush. Press firmly in place and hold for one minute until the glue sets. Repeat for the other end panel. (See Figure 5-16.)

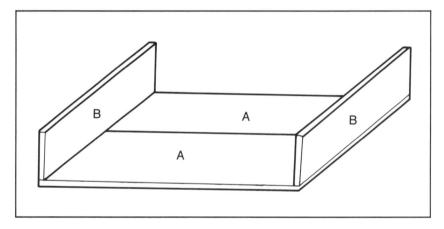

FIG. 5-16. *Attach the end panels to the box bottom.*

Detail from color plate 1.

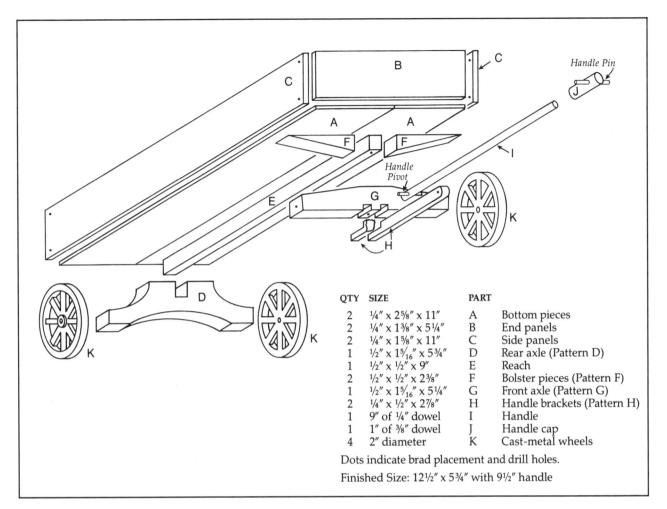

FIG. 5-17. *Express wagon assembly.*

QTY	SIZE	PART	
2	¼″ x 2⅝″ x 11″	A	Bottom pieces
2	¼″ x 1⅜″ x 5¼″	B	End panels
2	¼″ x 1⅝″ x 11″	C	Side panels
1	½″ x 1⁵⁄₁₆″ x 5¾″	D	Rear axle (Pattern D)
1	½″ x ½″ x 9″	E	Reach
2	½″ x ½″ x 2⅜″	F	Bolster pieces (Pattern F)
1	½″ x 1⁵⁄₁₆″ x 5¼″	G	Front axle (Pattern G)
2	¼″ x ½″ x 2⅞″	H	Handle brackets (Pattern H)
1	9″ of ¼″ dowel	I	Handle
1	1″ of ⅜″ dowel	J	Handle cap
4	2″ diameter	K	Cast-metal wheels

Dots indicate brad placement and drill holes.

Finished Size: 12½″ x 5¾″ with 9½″ handle

3. Turn the box assembly on its side and evenly apply glue to the three edges (bottom and ends). Align a side panel on the glued edges (all edges flush) and hold firmly in place for one minute. Repeat for the other side. To secure, nail two ½″ brads (hold them with long-nose pliers) through the side panels into the ends at all four corners. (See Figure 5-17 for placement.) Turn the box over and drive four evenly spaced ½″ brads through the bottom into each end panel.

CONSTRUCTING THE UNDERCARRIAGE
(Refer to Figure 5-17)

1. Transfer the rear axle pattern (D), page 104, to the ½″ pine; cut and sand. Drill one ¹⁄₁₆″ centered hole in each end to a depth of approximately ⅝″ for the wheel nails.

2. From the ½″ pine, cut one piece ½″ x 9″ for the reach (E). Sand. Drill a centered ¹⁄₁₆″ hole ¼″ from one end.

3. Transfer the bolster pattern (F) to the ½″ pine and cut two bolster pieces; sand.

4. Put some glue in the slot of the rear axle and set the nondrilled end of the reach in the slot. Allow the glue to dry.

5. Paint pieces D, E, and F black, but *do not paint* the areas that will be glued to the box (see Figure 5-17) because paint on a glued surface will weaken the bond. Let the paint dry. Apply an even coat of glue to the unpainted surfaces of the reach and rear axle. Center the assembly on the bottom of the box. Press firmly and hold in place for one minute until the glue sets.

6. Turn the box over (support the front end with a block of wood to level the wagon) and drive two ¾″ brads through the bottom of the box into the rear axle, one on each side.

7. Turn the wagon over and glue the bolster pieces in place. Press firmly and hold until the glue sets.

(Text continues on page 105.)

Express Wagon Wood Pattern Pieces

Dotted lines indicate drill guidelines.

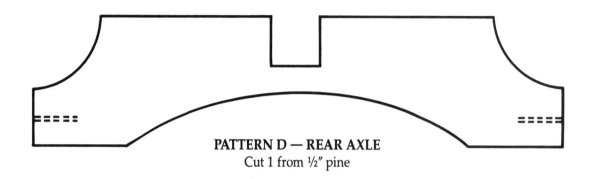

PATTERN D — REAR AXLE
Cut 1 from ½″ pine

PATTERN F — BOLSTER
Cut 2 from ½″ pine

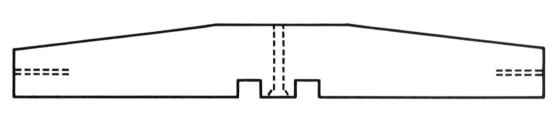

PATTERN G — FRONT AXLE
Cut from ½″ pine

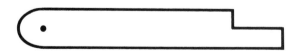

PATTERN H — HANDLE BRACKET
Cut 2 from ¼″ x 1⅜″ lattice

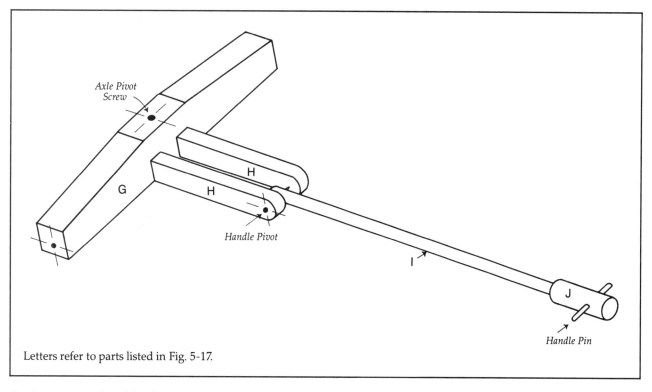

Axle Pivot
Screw

G

H

H

Handle Pivot

I

J

Handle Pin

Letters refer to parts listed in Fig. 5-17.

FIG. 5-18. *Front axle and handle assembly.*

CONSTRUCTING THE FRONT AXLE AND HANDLE
(Refer to Figure 5-18)

1. Transfer the front axle pattern (G) to the ½″ pine; cut and sand. Drill one 1/16″ hole in each end to a depth of approximately ⅝″ for the wheel nails. Drill a 5/32″ hole for the axle pivot screw on the underside of the front axle, centered between the slots. Countersink the hole, using a No. 8 counterbore bit.

2. Transfer the handle bracket pattern (H) to the 1⅜″ lattice and cut. You will need two, so repeat this step. Drill a 1/16″ hole through each piece (the drill hole is indicated on the pattern piece). Apply glue to the slots in the front axle and insert the handle brackets. Secure by nailing each with a ½″ brad.

3. Drill a 1/16″ hole ¼″ from one end of the 9″ dowel for the handle (I). Sand.

4. Drill a 5/64″ hole through the 1″ length of ⅜″ dowel, ¼″ from one end. This piece is the handle cap (J). Holding the piece securely with pliers, drill a centered ¼″ hole in the other end. (NOTE: To help control centering, drill with progressively larger bits. Start with 1/16″, then use 5/32″, and finish with ¼″.)

5. Using the wire-cutter part of the long-nose pliers, cut off both ends of the 6d finishing nail (leaving an approximate size of 1¼″). Round the ends with medium-grit sandpaper. Insert this pin into the handle cap and adjust it until it is centered.

6. Using the wire-cutter part of the long-nose pliers, cut ½″ off the pointed end of the 1¼″ brad. Insert the handle (I) between the brackets (H). To prevent damage to the fragile brackets while hammering the brad (pivot), support the brackets by placing the handle cap between them. Resting one bracket on a flat surface, drive the brad through the top bracket and the handle and into the other bracket.

7. Glue the handle cap to the handle. Paint the axle and handle black.

PAINTING AND STENCILING THE WAGON

1. Use the 1″ sponge brush to paint the outside of the wagon Red Clay and the inside black (for a time-worn finish, thin the paint with water and paint with a wash). Let the paint dry.

2. Measure in ⅛″ from the edge of the side panel and draw a light pencil line all the way around that edge. Using a No. 1 round brush and a steady hand, paint a thin (1/16″) black stripe over the pencil line (the paint will flow more easily if it is thinned with extender). If you're not comfortable hand-painting the stripe, go over the pencil guideline with a ruler and a fine black felt-tip marker. Repeat on the other side panel.

(Text continues on next page.)

Express Wagon Stencil

3. To make stencils, trace "EXPRESS" and the corner design onto Mylar (a separate piece for each) and cut them out. (If desired, simply hand-paint "EXPRESS" on the side panels or print it, using the black marker.) Center the "EXPRESS" stencil on a side panel (just below the top stripe and 2¼" from the wagon edge); tape it in place and stencil it Harvest Gold. Stencil the design in each corner Harvest Gold. Repeat on the other side panel.

PUTTING IT TOGETHER

1. Use a 1¼" No. 6 flat-head wood screw (the axle pivot screw) to attach the front axle assembly to the wagon, first placing two No. 6 flat washers between the axle and the reach. Tighten, then adjust enough to allow free movement.

2. Antique the wheels, if desired, before attaching them (see Chapter 1, page 21). Place a No. 6 flat washer between each wheel and the axle. Attach each using a 1" black paneling nail. Hold the front axle firmly while nailing to prevent any damage. The wheels should rotate freely.

6
Gameboards: Pastimes from the Past

EFORE THE advent of radio, television, and other modern-day modes of entertainment, our ancestors spent many pleasurable hours playing board games. Wintry weather or a visit to the general store was good reason for a game of Parcheesi or checkers. Prior to the 1850s, the majority of the boards they played on were handcrafted (usually by the male in the family) from pine and painted with oils. Like the beautiful pieced quilts made by the women of that time, many of these gameboards were carefully made and imaginatively decorated — outstanding examples of American folk art. Many were distinguished by their bold graphic designs and beautiful color combinations, while others were hand-painted with simple geometric shapes or a trailing floral or animal border. Some were carved in relief, possibly to enable the players to enjoy the game in a dimly lit room. Because of this individuality and their symbolic characterization of an era with an unhurried enjoyment of life, antique gameboards have become a very popular (and expensive) collectible, holding a place of honor in many folk art collections.

The reproduction gameboards found in this chapter can be a much-admired decorating accessory in a contemporary or country-style home. Their striking designs and beautiful patchwork colors combine to create a stunning focal point when displayed alone or as a wall grouping. Or better yet, why not gather the family around, turn off the television, and settle in for an evening of old-fashioned fun.

NOTE: Hand-painting and stenciling techniques are used to create these boards; refer to Chapter 1 for painting tips and Chapter 4 for stenciling tips.

The Basic Checkerboard

THESE instructions are for a very simple, unadorned checkerboard. You can create any of the other checkerboards by following these basic instructions with only slight variations. There's no need to measure and hand-paint each square; the checkerboard stencil (made in step 3) will allow you to stencil the sixty-four squares quickly and easily. Any number of color combinations can be used on this board; some attractive choices are antique white with red or blue squares, blue with red squares, or a stained board with black or red squares. Whichever board you choose to make, you will need all the materials listed in the supply list; so as not to be repetitious, only materials needed in addition to those will be listed later.

SUPPLIES
20″ length of 1″ x 12″ pine
Sandpaper (medium and fine)
1″ sponge brush, large stencil brush
Acrylic paint or stain
Paper plate, paper towels
Ruler, pencil
6″ x 11⅜″ sheet of Mylar, X-acto knife, pane of glass, masking tape
Band or crosscut saw

OPTIONAL SUPPLIES
Sealer and brush
Antiquing glaze and spray matte acrylic sealer
7′ length of ¼″ x 1⅛″ lattice (for the frame and dividers)
Twenty-two ¾″ wire brads
Hammer
Wood filler

Detail from color plate 3.

MAKING THE BASIC CHECKERBOARD

1. Sand the board and seal it (this step is optional — do not seal if you plan to use stain). Using the 1″ sponge brush, stain the board or basecoat it with two or three thin coats of paint. Let the paint dry between coats. (If the paint is applied too heavily, ridges might appear when it is dry.)

2. Measure 4½″ from each end of the board and draw a light pencil line from one side to the other. You now have a 4½″ tray at each end and an 11″ center playing area.

3. Tape Mylar over the checkerboard pattern, leaving a 1″ margin on all sides of the pattern. Transfer all lines, including the placement lines, to the Mylar. Place the Mylar on a pane of glass and cut out the eight squares.

4. You will be stenciling a total of eight rows (four stenciled squares per row), two rows at a time. Begin by stenciling rows 1 and 3. Align the right side placement line of the stencil on the right side of the board, placing the top placement line on the pencil line you drew in step 2. Tape the Mylar in place and stencil eight squares. (See Figure 6-1.) To stencil rows 2 and 4, drop the stencil down one row and shift it to the left side of the board (edge aligned with the left side placement line), match the bottom corners of the stenciled squares with the top corners of the stencil openings, and stencil. (See Figure 6-2.) You now have half the squares stenciled. To complete the other half, once again shift the stencil to the

FIG. 6-1. *Stenciling rows 1 and 3.*

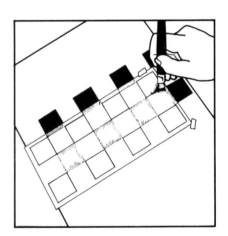

FIG. 6-2. *Stenciling rows 2 and 4.*

right side of the board, match the top corners of the (first row) stencil openings with the bottom corners of the fourth row of stenciled squares. Tape the Mylar in place and stencil rows 5 and 7. To complete, drop the stencil down one row and shift it to the left edge, align the corners of the squares, tape it in place, and stencil rows 6 and 8.

(Text continues on page 110.)

Basic Checkerboard Stencil

Cut out solid squares.

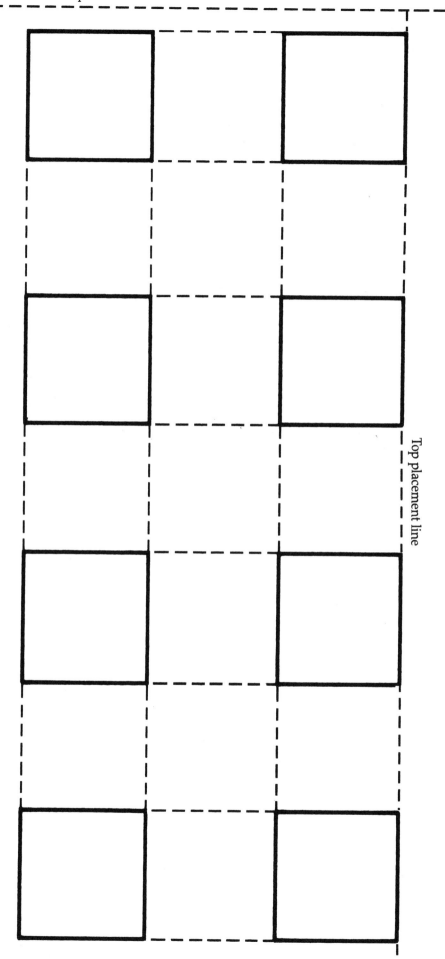

Left side placement line

Top placement line

Right side placement line

5. Gameboards look best with a mellow, aged finish. If desired, antique your board, following the suggestions in Chapter 1 (page 20). If you are going to use an antiquing glaze, be certain to spray the painted surface with a matte acrylic sealer beforehand. This will prevent the paint from being rubbed off as you apply the glaze.

FRAMING THE BOARD

NOTE: As an alternative to framing, simply paint the side edges a matching or contrasting color.

1. Cut two 20½" side pieces. Then measure the width of the checkerboard to determine the length of the end pieces and dividers. Cut two end pieces from the ¼" x 1⅛" lattice. Cut another piece of lattice the same length and from it cut two ⅜"-wide strips for the dividers (thin strips of wood separating the trays from the center playing area).

2. Paint or stain all the pieces and set them aside.

3. Evenly space and set the brads ⅜" from the edge of the lattice as follows: five brads in each side piece, three in each end piece, and three in each divider (on the ¼" edge, not the ⅜" side, since the dividers will be attached standing on edge). (See Figure 6-3.) Drive the brads so that the points are just visible on the other side.

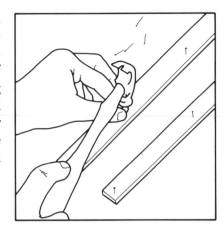

FIG. 6-3. *Set the brads in the framing sides.*

4. Place the gameboard on a flat surface, position a side piece extending beyond the board ¼" at each end, and nail it in place. (See Figure 6-4.) Repeat for the other side. Hold the gameboard on end and nail each end in place. Attach the dividers.

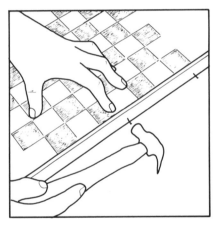

FIG. 6-4. *Nail the side pieces to the board.*

5. Countersink the brads using a larger nail (see Chapter 1, page 19), fill the holes with wood filler, and paint or stain over them.

MAKING THE CHECKERS

Now that you've got the board, all you need is the checkers! For a quick-and-easy, rustic-looking set, search your woodpile for a 1' length of tree branch (diameter about ¾"). Using a handsaw or band saw, slice the branch into twenty-four ¼" thick checkers. Paint them all or leave half of them natural. For a really unusual set, paint or stencil a design element from the board onto each. Years ago, checkers were made in the same way from corncobs (see Sun and Moon Checkerboard, page 111). For a modern version, substitute a dowel for the branch.

Sun and Moon Checkerboard

THIS charming board is a reproduction of a late-nineteenth-century design. The tray designs are hand-painted and the squares stenciled. Refer to the basic checkerboard instructions on page 108 as you work. The supplies listed below are in addition to those listed there.

SUPPLIES
No. 4 flat bristle brush, No. 1 round brush
Acrylic paint (Folk Art colors: Taffy, black, Coastal Blue, Lemonade, Cinnamon, Burgundy)
Two 5″ x 11″ sheets of tracing paper
5″ x 11″ sheet of graphite paper
Raw umber and black oil paints and turpentine for antiquing glaze, cloth

MAKING THE BOARD

1. Make the board and section it as described in steps 1 and 2 of The Basic Checkerboard, page 108.

2. Paint the center section Taffy; let it dry. Stencil the squares black (stencil lightly, letting the board show through at the center of each square).

3. With the sponge brush, paint the tray ends Coastal Blue. Trace the end patterns onto tracing paper, sandwich the same-size piece of graphite paper between the tracing paper and the board, tape everything in place, and transfer the designs to the trays.

Paint the sun Lemonade. Dry-brush the rays with quick, light, outward strokes of the bristle brush (you don't want an opaque look); let it dry. Dry-brush some Cinnamon-colored rays between the others. Paint the half-circle marks Burgundy and Cinnamon.

Paint the stars, the quarter-moons, and the full moon Lemonade. Outline the full moon with Cinnamon; before it dries, use the edge of your flat brush to blend some of the Cinnamon into the Lemonade, giving the moon a more rounded appearance. Thin the black paint with water and paint the face on the moon.

4. Spray the board with matte acrylic sealer. Mix equal parts of raw umber oil paint and turpentine, add a small amount of black oil paint, and blend until you get a consistency of light cream. Dip a corner of the cloth into the glaze and rub it along the sides of the board. Then, using a circular motion, rub it around the edges and corners of the tray to mute the colors and darken the sky area (to give the impression that the sun is rising from a dark sky). Blend well for a soft, subtle look.

5. Paint the frame pieces and the dividers with a black wash (see Chapter 1, page 11) or omit the dividers and outline the playing area with a thin (⅛″) line of black paint. Attach all pieces as explained in steps 3–5 of Framing the Board, page 110.

Detail from color plate 1.

Sun and Moon
Checkerboard

TOP PANEL DESIGN

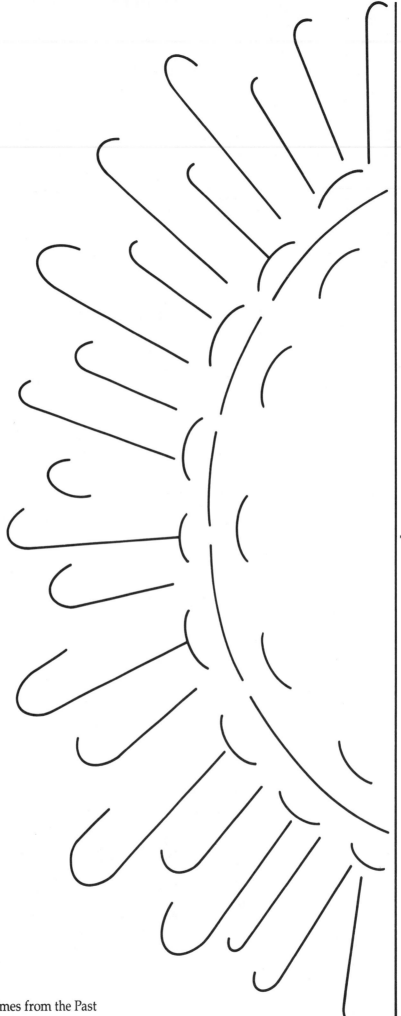

This line butts to checkerboard pattern.

Sun and Moon
Checkerboard

BOTTOM PANEL DESIGN

This line butts to checkerboard pattern.

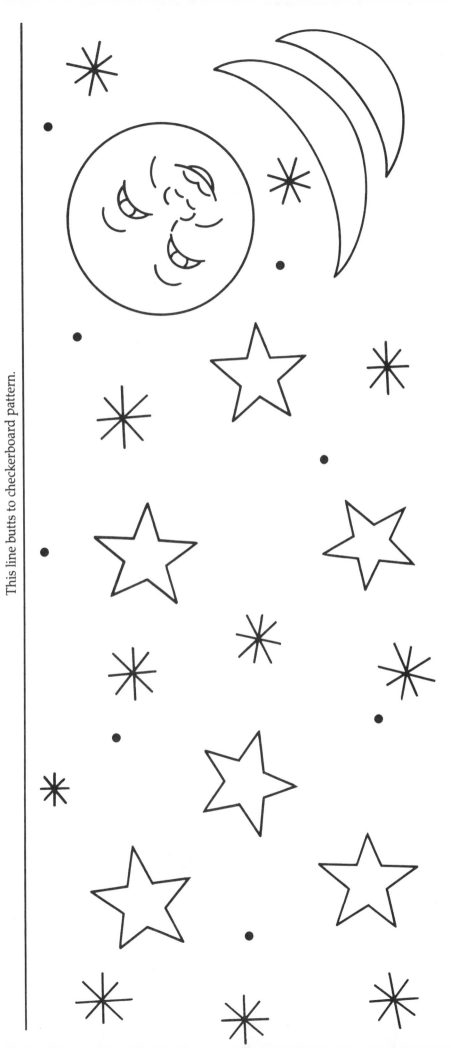

Double Hearts Checkerboard

ALL the designs on this board are stenciled, but they can be hand-painted, if you prefer. Transfer the design with graphite paper, turn the pattern over for the other half, and paint, using the colors given for stenciling or the colors of your choice. Refer to the basic checkerboard instructions on page 108 as you work. The supplies listed below are in addition to those listed there.

SUPPLIES
Acrylic paint (Folk Art colors: Taffy, Paisley Blue, Calico Red, black, Clover, white)
6″ x 7½″ sheet of Mylar
Small stencil brushes
Toothpick or stylus
Burnt umber oil paint and turpentine for antiquing glaze, cloth

MAKING THE BOARD

1. Make the board and section it as described in steps 1 and 2 of The Basic Checkerboard, page 108. Paint both end trays Taffy. When the trays are dry, mark the center of each (from top to bottom) with a light pencil line. Leave the center playing section unpainted; this will be antiqued in step 5.

2. Stencil the squares black.

3. Transfer the half pattern to the Mylar (mark the centerline) and cut it out. Since all the colors will be painted using the same stencil, mask off the surrounding openings for colors other than the one you are using.

4. Center the stencil on one end of the board. Tape it in place and stencil the birds: head and tail, Paisley Blue; wing, Calico Red; beak and feet, black. Stencil the stems and leaves Clover and the small flowers white. Dip a stylus or the end of a toothpick into black and paint the small dots in the center of each flower and an eye for the bird. Make small white dots on the corner stem designs. Clean and dry the stencil. Turn it over and center it on the other half of the board; tape it in place. Stencil the same as for the first half. Repeat all the stenciling steps on the other end tray.

5. Spray the board with matte acrylic sealer. Mix equal parts of burnt umber oil paint and turpentine. With a sponge brush, spread a thin coat on the center (checkered) section of the board. Then, with a clean cloth, wipe the surface to remove enough of the glaze to give a pleasing color to the wood. Dip a corner of the cloth into the glaze and, using a circular motion, lightly antique the edges of the end panels (1″ to 2″ in). If the color becomes too dark, dip a cloth in turpentine and remove the excess glaze. You might have to repaint the white flowers after antiquing.

6. Antique the frame pieces with the same glaze. Attach all pieces as explained in steps 3–5 of Framing the Board, page 110.

Detail from color plate 9.

Double Hearts
Checkerboard

HALF PATTERN FOR STENCIL

FLOWER PETALS — white

DOTS — black

HEAD AND TAIL — Paisley Blue

BEAK AND FEET — black

WING — Calico Red

Centerline

STEMS AND LEAVES — Clover

Flowers and Vines Checkerboard

THE striking simplicity of this reproduction nineteenth-century game-board is what makes it so appealing and so easy to make. The board is hand-painted using only two main colors: red and black. Refer to the basic checkerboard instructions on page 108 as you work. The supplies listed below are in addition to those listed there.

SUPPLIES
Acrylic paint (Folk Art colors: black, Calico Red, Paisley Blue)
5″ x 11″ sheet of tracing and graphite paper
Extender
No. 1 round brush, No. 2 flat brush

MAKING THE BOARD

1. Make the board as described in step 1 of The Basic Checkerboard, page 108.

2. Paint both sides and all the edges of the board with a black wash (see Chapter 1, page 11), and let it dry. Basecoat one side of the board with two thin coats of Calico Red and let it dry.

3. Section the board as in step 2 of The Basic Checkerboard, page 108.

4. Stencil the squares black.

5. Trace the pattern design onto tracing paper and transfer it onto the end panels with graphite paper. Blend some black paint (or Paisley Blue) with extender and water (so the paint will flow more smoothly) and paint the stems and leaves with the No. 1 round brush. To facilitate painting the thin lines of the stems, fill all the bristles of the brush with paint, rolling the brush to a point as you lift it out of the paint. Paint the flowers with the same black paint, using the flat brush.

6. To highlight the checkered playing field, mask off a ¼″ strip on all sides of it with tape (the tape will overlap the squares slightly along the sides). Stencil this strip Paisley Blue. If desired, spray with matte acrylic sealer and mute the colors by antiquing with a raw umber–black–turpentine glaze (see Chapter 1, page 20). Round the corners of the board by sanding them with medium-grit paper.

Detail from color plate 5.

**Flowers and Vines
Checkerboard Pattern**

This line butts to checkerboard pattern.

Parcheesi Board

SUPPLIES
19″ x 19″ piece of ¼″ plywood
Crosscut or band saw
Square
Sandpaper (medium and fine)
½″ masking tape
Stain (English Oak), cloth, hide glue
  for crackle finish (optional)
Acrylic paint (Folk Art colors: Taffy,
  Shamrock, Golden Harvest,
  Cinnamon, Raspberry Wine, Coffee
  Bean, black)
Paper plate, paper towels
One 1″ and two 2″ sponge brushes,
  three stencil brushes, No. 1 round
  and No. 1 flat brushes
Yardstick, pencil, compass
Two 8″ x 8″ sheets of Mylar, X-acto
  knife, pane of glass
Spray matte acrylic sealer
Burnt umber oil paint and turpentine
  for antiquing glaze, cloth
8′ length of ½″ quarter-round molding
  (for the frame)
Miter box
Twenty ⅝″ wire brads, hammer
Wood glue
Wood filler

THE history of Parcheesi, often referred to as the royal game of India, can be traced back more than twelve hundred years. In sixteenth-century India Parcheesi is known to have been played by the emperor, with his courtyard as a giant gameboard and female servants as the pawns. Less prosperous Indians enjoyed the game on boards made from decorated cloth. From there, this ancient game of luck and skill was brought to England and eventually to America, where it has remained a favorite game for generations. The bright colors and graphic designs on this reproduction nineteenth-century board combine to create a beautiful, quilt-like appearance. The corner designs on the original board were undoubtedly drawn with a compass and then painstakingly hand-painted. You can accomplish the same look in a fraction of the time with stenciling. A crackle finish can be used to mimic the crazing of old paint so often seen on antique boards. (This finish is optional; if you choose not to use it, omit step 2 below and basecoat the board Taffy.)

PREPARING THE BOARD

1. It is important that you cut and square the plywood to exactly 19″ x 19″. All measurements will be off if you start with an irregular size. Sand the board and then mask off a ½″ border on all sides with ½″ masking tape.

2. If you plan to use a crackle finish, you might want to try the technique on a small piece of scrap wood before doing the board. Stain the board and let it dry. (Use a medium-shade oil- or water-based stain; I used Red Devil English Oak.) Thin the hide glue with water (2 parts glue to 1 part water). Use a sponge brush to coat the board evenly with a thin layer of glue. Let it dry completely, ten to twenty-four hours (if the humidity is high or the weather wet, it may take longer). Place enough Taffy paint on your palette to cover the board. Dip a 2″ sponge brush in the paint and, working quickly (crackling will begin as soon as the paint is

applied), apply an even coat, brushing from top to bottom. Take care not to overlap the strokes; it can result in a blotchy, uneven look. Let the paint dry.

3. Divide the unmasked 18″ square center section into nine 6″ squares and mark with light pencil lines. Mark the exact center of each corner square (for how to find a center point, see Chapter 1, page 13). Set the compass to a radius of 3″. (Since accuracy is important, measure the distance between the point and the pencil to make sure it is 3″.) Place the point of the compass on the center dot of each corner square and draw a circle. The circle should just graze all four sides of the square. Divide each of the four remaining outside squares into three columns, each column measuring 2″ wide and 6″ long. All the columns should extend lengthwise from the center square. (See Figure 6-5.)

Detail from color plate 4.

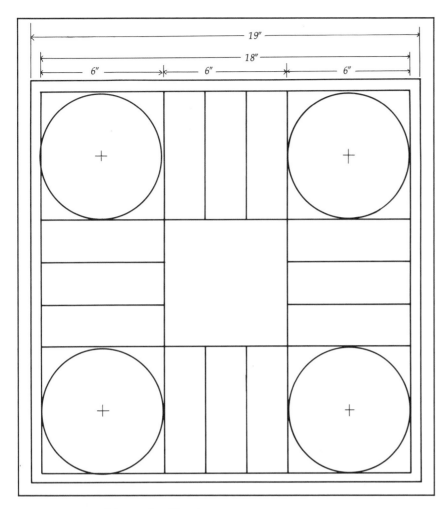

FIG. 6-5. *Layout of the Parcheesi board.*

3. Stencil the center column of each outside block Cinnamon. To be sure of making clean, sharp edges, hold a piece of cardboard along the edge as you stencil or place masking tape on each pencil line (Figure 6-6). Allow the paint to dry, then divide the columns in each of the four blocks into ¾″ spaces (eight spaces per column, twenty-four spaces per block) and mark with light pencil lines. Use a No. 1 flat brush to paint the bottom space (on the outside edge of the board) in each center column Harvest Gold (thinned). Thin some black paint with water to get a light gray and paint the fourth space from the bottom in each side column. With the round brush, paint a Raspberry Wine circle the size of a dime in the center of each gold and gray space. (See Figure 6-7.)

(Text continues on page 121.)

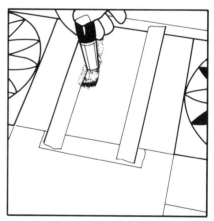

FIG. 6-6. *Mask off the center column for stenciling.*

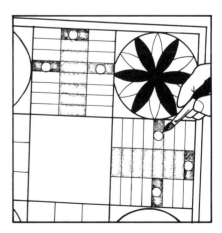

FIG. 6-7. *Paint a circle in each gold and gray space.*

PAINTING AND STENCILING

1. The corner design will be cut as a two-part color-separated stencil. Tape one sheet of Mylar over the pattern (page 120) and trace all the light areas of the design with a solid line; trace all the dark areas with a broken line. Transfer the centerline at the top and trace the circle around the design; label this stencil A – green. Tape the second sheet of Mylar over the first, edges even, and trace all the dark areas of the design with a solid line and all the light areas with a broken line. Transfer the centerline at the top, trace the circle around the design, and label this stencil B – red. With an X-acto knife cut along the solid lines of the design inside the circle on each stencil — don't cut out the circle.

2. Paint each circle with a wash of Harvest Gold. Let it dry. Center and tape stencil A on a circle and stencil it Shamrock. Repeat for the other three circles. Align stencil B over a previously stenciled area, matching the broken lines on the stencil with the stenciled design. Stencil with Raspberry Wine. Repeat for the remaining circles.

Parcheesi Board Corner Stencil

NOTE: Centerpoint of stencil may be reinforced with a small piece of transparent tape if necessary.

Top

Transfer for Center Block

4. Paint the center square with a wash of Harvest Gold. When it is dry, measure in 1" from all sides and mark. Mask the edges with cardboard or masking tape (Figure 6-8) and stencil this strip with Coffee Bean. Use the round brush to rim the edges with a thin (⅛") line of black. Transfer "HOME" from the pattern to the center of the board with graphite paper (or freehand) and paint it with Cinnamon. Remove the masking tape from the edges. Use the thinned black paint and the No. 1 round brush to paint over the pencil lines on the outside edge of the playing field, across the columns, and around the circles in the corner designs (the line should be about ⅛"). (See Figure 6-9.) Don't worry if the lines are less than perfect; you aren't striving for a machine-made look.

FIG. 6-8. *Stencil a 1" strip around the edge of the center square.*

FINISHING

1. Erase all visible pencil marks. Spray the board with matte acrylic sealer. For the antiquing glaze, mix equal parts of burnt umber oil paint and turpentine. Lightly antique the board (if it becomes too dark, remove the excess glaze with a cloth moistened with turpentine). Wrap a cloth around your finger, dip it in straight burnt umber, and antique the edges of the board a shade darker.

2. Miter-cut four 19" lengths of ½" quarter-round molding. The rounded side will be on the inside of the board. Antique each piece with the burnt umber glaze. Set five ⅝" wire brads in the rounded side of each piece, 3/16" from the outside edge (the points should be just visible on the other side). Place each piece on the gameboard and check for fit; trim as needed. Remove, noting the side from which each piece came. Spread glue evenly on each piece (only on the side that will rest on the gameboard) and attach it to its fitted location on the board; nail it in place. Countersink the nails (see Chapter 1, page 19) and fill the holes with wood filler. Antique the filler to blend with the frame.

FIG. 6-9. *Final Parcheesi board.*

7
Whittling
and
Carving

THE EARLIEST settlers arrived in America with few personal belongings, resulting in a shortage of many things. But with the seemingly endless expanse of virgin forests, wood was always plentiful. So out of necessity, the Colonists carved. From this bountiful natural resource, they fashioned everything from the walls that sheltered them to their eating utensils. People of all ages became adept at this craft. As metals, glass, and ceramics became more accessible and took the place of wood for many practical items, the carver turned his attention from the functional to the decorative. Carving thrived as both a business and a hobby. Examples of this rich history of carving still abound in the form of carousel horses, ship figureheads, wooden sculptures, shop figures, and elaborate carvings on wainscoting, mantels, and doors. On a less grandiose scale, amateur carvers and whittlers produced many one-of-a-kind toys, whirligigs, whimseys, and decoys.

Wilhelm Schimmel, an itinerant Pennsylvania German, was one of America's most colorful and legendary folk art carvers. He traveled the Cumberland countryside, trading his carvings for a night's lodging or a meal, from the 1860s until his death in a Pennsylvania almshouse in 1890. He was extremely prolific; in the last twenty-five years of his life he created well over five hundred carvings, mainly of small birds, animals, and figures. He is best known for his eagles, some of which have a wingspan of over three feet. His distinctive impressionistic pieces rank among the most coveted finds for a folk art collector today, and examples of his work can be seen in our most prestigious museums.

Carving and whittling, unlike some crafts, did not disappear with the coming of the Industrial Revolution. In fact, they seemed to flourish because of it. They were then, as they are today, relaxing and satisfying crafts, which for the cost of a knife and a piece of wood open the door to a world of self-expression.

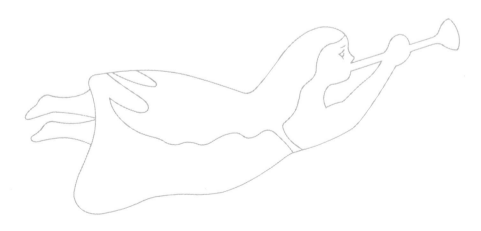

How to Whittle and Carve

THE terms *whittling* and *carving* are often used synonymously, but there is a distinction. Whittling is done primarily by holding the wood in one hand while chipping away at it with a knife held in the opposite hand; carving usually involves the use of gouges or chisels to remove wood from a board often clamped to a workbench. However, I will be speaking only of carving in its general sense throughout this chapter. For the projects in this chapter, you will need a saber, band, or coping saw to rough out the patterns and a knife for carving.

The best woods to use for the projects in this chapter are knot-free white pine (clear pine), sugar pine, poplar, and basswood. Pine and poplar can be found at most lumberyards, while basswood can usually be found in a hobby or craft shop (or it can be ordered through one of the companies listed under Wood and Woodworking Supplies in the Source Guide on page 159). Each of these woods is soft and light colored, with a fine, closed grain, making it ideal for carving. Because green wood tends to warp and split as it dries, choose only well-seasoned wood.

Hardwoods can be used, but just as the name implies, they are hard, dense, and much more difficult to work with (see Chapter 1, page 17). They are best left to an experienced carver using a mallet and chisel. Each type of wood handles differently when carved; the more open the grain, for example, the more likely the wood is to split. When selecting a piece of wood for carving, always look for straightness of grain and even color. Color variations often signal changes in hardness. Experiment until you find the type of wood you're most comfortable using.

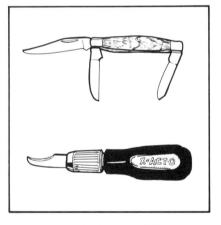

FIG. 7-1. *Pocketknife (top) and X-acto carving knife (bottom).*

CARVING TOOLS
(See Figure 7-1)

X-acto knife: I prefer to use an X-acto carving knife, which is sold as a handle with a variety of disposable blades. The fact that the blades (which are extremely sharp) are replaceable and quite inexpensive makes this a versatile tool and eliminates the need to sharpen blades (a feature I really appreciate). Although you can purchase many different carving blades to fit the handle, use the concave blade (No. 262004) for the projects in this chapter. This tool can be found in most hobby shops, or it can be ordered through the Dick Blick Company (see the Source Guide on page 159).

Jackknife: A good quality jackknife or pocketknife with a carbon-steel blade will get you started. Make sure it has two to three blades for cutting versatility, and a sturdy handle at least 3" long. This type of knife must be sharpened periodically with a whetstone or Carborundum stone. A blade used continually on softwood should hold its edge for a day or two.

Whichever knife you choose, it is of utmost importance that you keep the blade razor sharp at all times. Dull blades are responsible for more slips and injuries than sharp blades.

LAYING OUT PATTERNS

Wood carving is easier and the resulting piece stronger when carving is done with the grain. Therefore, it is important to place the length of the pattern piece along the grain of the wood. For instance, the Uncle Sam Whirligig (page 129) would look foolish and be extremely difficult to carve if placed across the grain, so it must be laid out vertically on the board. The main direction of the Angel Weather Vane (page 126) is side to side, so it should be placed horizontally on the board with the grain running from the boot to the horn.

Lay your pattern out on the wood and trace around the outline, then use a saber, band, or coping saw (or the straight cut described on page 124) to remove the large areas of excess wood. Then your piece will be ready for the finer carving strokes. It's helpful to keep a clear image of what you are carving in your mind at all times. Many carvers have said that they feel as though they are releasing some imprisoned thing or being from the wood. I think that's a great way to approach a carving project.

BASIC CARVING STROKES

The following basic carving strokes will see you through any number of projects quite successfully. One of the most important things to remember when carving is always to carve *with* the grain, but not *in* the grain. There is a difference. If you cut exactly in the direction of the grain, the wood is likely to split. When cutting with the grain, you will actually be carving at a very slight angle to the direction of the grain, thereby preventing splits. Start out with slow, shallow strokes. If at some point the knife seems to catch in the wood, possibly causing a split, stop. Turn the piece of wood around and cut to the same point from the opposite direction.

At times it will be necessary to carve across the grain. The wood is much harder to carve this way, so work slowly, with short, shaving strokes. To get a feel for the wood and the knife you're using, practice the following cuts on some scrap wood before starting the projects. Remember, the best teacher is practice!

Straight cut: This is a rough cut and is good for removing large pieces of wood when you are beginning a project. Be careful, though: Because of the position of the knife, you will not have complete control over the cut and could slice off too long a piece. Hold the wood with one hand (*behind* the knife); with your other hand, grip the knife firmly and cut *away from you* with a downward motion, directing the stroke with the muscles of your arm. (See Figure 7-2.) For more control, brace the knife with your thumb.

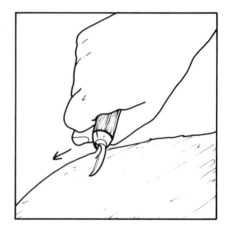

FIG. 7-2. *The straight cut.*

Paring cut: As its name implies, this cut is similar to that used to peel vegetables. The versatile paring cut gives you excellent control over the blade and is especially useful for carving curved areas and small pieces. If you're right-handed, support the wood with your left hand, hold the knife tightly in your right hand, and draw the knife toward you while bracing the carved area with your right thumb. (See Figure 7-3.) In the beginning, it's a good idea to cover your right thumb with an adhesive bandage or rubber fingertip (from an office supply store) to protect it from possible knife slips.

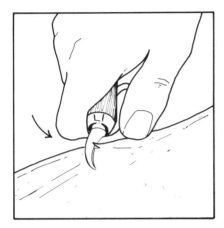

FIG. 7-3. *The paring cut.*

Thumb-assist: Hold the knife in one hand and use the thumb on the other hand to guide and push the blade away from you. Because your thumb is used as a guide, this is a well-controlled cut and is excellent when short, precise cuts are needed. It's also good for shaving and smoothing the wood. (See Figure 7-4.)

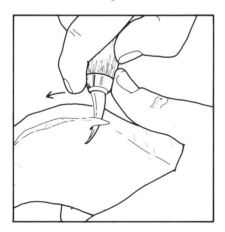

FIG. 7-4. *The thumb-assist.*

V-cut: A well-controlled cut used to notch away portions of wood, this is especially useful in small, cramped areas (such as between legs or under arms) where a sweeping stroke cannot be used. Again, using your thumb for control, hold the knife with the other hand and force the blade into the wood at an angle, cutting as deep as desired. Then, from the opposite direction, make a similar cut to complete the V-notch, making sure the cuts meet. (See Figure 7-5.) The chunk of wood should fall away easily; do not try to pop it out, or you might split the wood.

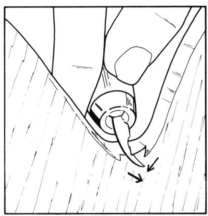

FIG. 7-5. *The V-cut.*

FINISHING

The appearance of some wood projects is enhanced by retaining most of the facets (whittle marks) left by the tool. Others look better if some or all of the facets are removed. The choice is yours. If you wish to remove some of the whittle marks, sand the item gently with a piece of slightly worn sandpaper or simply smooth the rough spots with the edge of your blade. For heavy sanding or to remove all traces of whittle marks, start with a medium-grit paper and finish with a very fine paper. Always sand with the grain.

When sanding on a curved surface or between legs, roll the sandpaper into a cylinder. For more frequent use, make a sanding stick by gluing (with contact cement) a small piece of sandpaper around a dowel. To make a sanding stick for flat surfaces, glue the paper around a ¼"-thick piece of wood.

Angel Weather Vane

SUPPLIES
22" x 28" piece of poster board,
  yardstick, pencil, scissors
25" length of 1" x 10" pine
Saber, band, or coping saw
Drill with ⁵⁄₁₆" bit
X-acto knife or jackknife
Sandpaper (medium and fine)
Tack cloth
Sealer (optional)
Acrylic paint (ivory, black, gold)
No. 10 flat brush, No. 2 round brush
Sawtooth picture hanger for hanging
  angel
5½" length of 2" x 6" pine, 14" length of
  ⁵⁄₁₆" dowel, drill with ⁵⁄₁₆" bit for
  freestanding angel

FOR OPTIONAL CRACKLE FINISH
Wood stain (oak or walnut)
Cloth
1", 2", and 3" sponge brushes
Hide glue
Gesso, paper plate

WEATHER vanes are avidly collected today for their appeal as decorative accessories. But in eighteenth- and nineteenth-century America, they served a more utilitarian purpose. Since the livelihood of so many people revolved around farming, it was of the utmost importance to have some indicator of impending weather conditions, no matter how vague that information might be. A boldly shaped weather vane, often placed on top of the tallest building in a community, served as a simple but reliable indicator of the direction of the wind.

Vanes were made from various materials. The earliest ones, handcrafted from wood in simple silhouette forms, were usually painted to enhance their visibility and protect them from the weather. Later, more elaborate, three-dimensional designs were manufactured from copper, iron, and tin. The design was often determined by location or the occupation of the maker; some even served as trade signs. Cocks, fish, and angels were commonly used on church steeples, while cows, horses, and sheep were a standby in farm settlements. In New England coastal villages, ships, gulls, and sea creatures were a popular motif. Many fine examples of these weather vanes still exist and can be seen in folk art museums and private collections.

This carved and painted angel is patterned after a late-nineteenth-century Massachusetts weather vane. Done in a silhouette style, this type of vane was often carved with chisels or cut out of flat planks with small saws. Because these vanes were meant to be seen from a distance, fine detail carving and painting was kept to a minimum. (The carving on this angel requires all the basic carving strokes, making it the perfect project for the beginning wood carver.) From prolonged exposure to the elements, the painted surface of these vanes often became cracked and crazed. I have included an optional technique to give your new vane that cracked, weathered look.

The original weather vane from which this pattern was derived is 27" long; the finished size of this one is about 24". If yours is to be used as a wall decoration, carve and finish only one side. If you want to make a freestanding piece, carve and paint both sides, then attach it to a wooden base with a dowel. (When using the crackle finish, one side must be completed and dry before you do the other.) Although this weather vane is especially suited to the Christmas season, its timeless Americana appeal makes it a perfect decorating accessory all year.

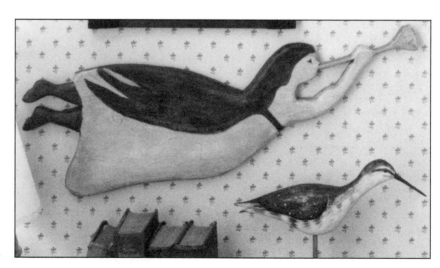

Detail from color plate 4.

MAKING THE WEATHER VANE

1. Enlarge the pattern on page 128 to scale (see Chapter 1, page 13), transfer the new pattern to the wood, and cut it out. If necessary, see Chapter 8, the bottom of page 141, for help in cutting the inner cutouts of the design.

2. Basically you will be rounding the edges of the angel, but do as little or as much carving as you like; this is an excellent project for practicing all the basic cuts. Begin by removing all hard edges, using the straight and thumb-assist strokes; round and smooth the edges with the paring stroke. Use the V-cut to remove wood from between the legs and between the hand and the horn. Trim the width and the depth of the horn slightly. If desired, round the arms and legs for a more three-dimensional look. This piece looks nice with the facets showing, so sand ever so lightly, then wipe with a tack cloth.

3. If you want to use the crackle finish, skip this paragraph and go to the next section. Otherwise, on a one-sided weather vane (for hanging on the wall), simply seal the wood, basecoat the back (ivory), then draw the painting lines on the front and paint as follows: hair, boots, and eye – black; horn – gold; dress and skin – ivory. If you are making a freestanding vane, draw the painting lines on both sides and paint. If desired, antique with a burnt umber glaze (Chapter 1, page 20).

MAKING A CRACKLE FINISH

1. Note that the design will be painted over the crackle finish. Before proceeding to the angel, try this technique on a piece of scrap wood. Begin by applying stain to the edges and both sides with a soft cloth. Allow it to dry.

2. Dip a 2″ sponge brush in water and squeeze it to remove excess moisture. Squeeze hide glue onto the angel and use the damp sponge brush to spread a thin, uniform coat of glue on the edges and one side. It's important that the entire surface be thoroughly coated with glue. Allow the glue to dry completely before proceeding. The glue should dry within twenty-four hours if it's applied in a dry indoor atmosphere; it might take longer on a humid day.

3. Pour about ½ cup of gesso on a paper plate. Although it is very thick and often difficult to spread, don't be tempted to thin it. Strive for an even distribution of gesso on all parts on the first application — *you cannot go over an area to even it out.* The crackling process begins immediately and would be covered over if you tried to rebrush the area.

Begin by applying the gesso to the edges of the angel with a 1″ sponge brush; then dip the 3″ sponge brush in gesso and, using long, sweeping strokes (going from feet to horn), apply it to the surface of the angel. (See Figure 7-6.) Do not overlap your strokes at any time! Allow the gesso to dry completely (one to two hours) before continuing. If you are making a two-sided, freestanding weather vane, repeat the process on the other side.

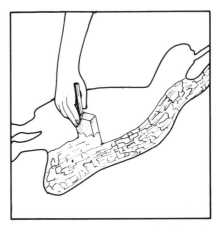

FIG. 7-6. *Applying a crackle finish to the angel weather vane.*

4. Transfer the painting lines to the angel. Thin the paint with water to an almost watercolor consistency and paint as described under Making the Weather Vane, step 3. If desired, antique with a burnt umber glaze (Chapter 1, page 20).

5. For a hanging angel, attach a sawtooth picture hanger to the center of the back. For a freestanding angel, use a 5⁄16″ bit to drill a hole ¾″ deep in the center of the base and the bottom edge of the angel. Attach with the dowel.

Angel Weather Vane Wood Pattern

One square equals 1″

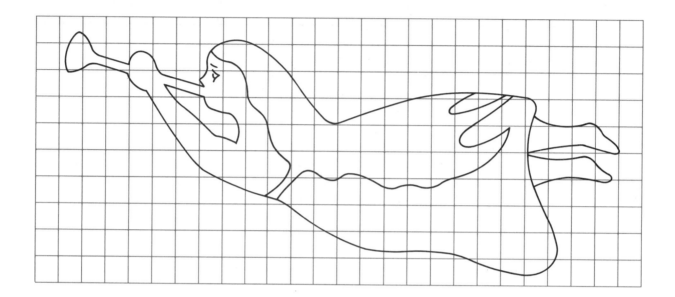

Uncle Sam Whirligig

SUPPLIES

16" length of ⁵⁄₄" x 4" pine
8" length of 1" x 4" pine
9" length of ³⁄₃₂" x 3" basswood
1⁵⁄₈" piece of 1⅛" dowel
½" piece of ⁵⁄₁₆" dowel
14" piece of ³⁄₁₆" dowel
Saber or band and coping saws
Square
Tape measure
Tracing and graphite paper, tape,
    pencil
Drill with ³⁄₃₂", ³⁄₁₆", ¹³⁄₆₄", and ⁵⁄₁₆" bits
Wood glue
Hammer
6" C-clamp
Sandpaper (medium and fine)
Tack cloth
X-acto knife or jackknife
Wax (paraffin or a candle)
Acrylic paint (Folk Art colors: Taffy,
    Wrought Iron, Red Clay, Apricot
    Cream, Honey Comb, Coffee Bean,
    Paisley Blue, white, black)
Paper plate, paper towels
No. 1 round and No. 6 flat brushes, 1"
    sponge brush
Extender
Two ³⁄₁₆" flat washers

Detail from color plate 1.

SIMPLY stated, according to Webster's, a whirligig is "a child's toy having a whirling motion." But there are two schools of thought as to what whirligigs were originally intended for. Some believe that they were a small weather vane, one meant to stand on a fence post or porch rail to whirl merrily in the breeze. Others believe they were meant to be a child's "Sunday toy" — a toy designed to delight and amuse quietly on a day set aside for worship and rest.

Many of the earliest examples of nineteenth-century whirligigs were the hand-carved, single-figure, arm-flailing variety. They were carved by amateurs, often to resemble soldiers or sailors. Their arms, usually mounted on a wooden or metal rod passing through the shoulders, held some sort of blade or paddle; sometimes the arms themselves were the blades. When placed in the wind or in the hand of a running child, the arms rotated rapidly. Later, more complex designs portrayed figures performing simple tasks: a woman churning butter, a man sawing wood, or a horse walking. These whirligigs, many of which were made from sheet metal or tin, were set in motion with propellers that turned gears and rods to make the figure move.

Whatever the style, whirligigs were always a unique expression of the maker's wit and creativity, and today they are among the most popular forms of American folk art. Unfortunately, since many were made of wood and were often battered by the weather, few of those made prior to 1850 survive today.

Although Uncle Sam's arms do whirl, he is not intended to be used as an out-of-doors working model; rather, he is designed to be a source of amusement and enjoyment inside your home. His body is whittled from white pine, and his arms, hat, and shoes are joined to the body with small wooden pegs and glue. His finished size is 6½" x 14¾". Uncle's whimsical yet stately qualities will endear him to all, and he's sure to become a welcome celebrant on every patriotic holiday.

MAKING THE BODY

NOTE: Since it is far easier and more accurate to drill into the flat side of a block of wood than a carved or rounded surface, drilling is done before carving whenever possible.

1. Cut an 11" length of ⁵⁄₄" x 4" pine, ends squared, from the 16" piece for the body; set aside the remaining 5" section for the base. For help in aligning the pattern (page 131), mark the center point at each end of the wood. Center and transfer the body pattern outline and the eyebrows, nose, and beard lines to the wood. To establish armhole locations on the body block, turn the block on edge and draw a line across the edge, 2⅝" from the top of the block. Using a square, continue to draw this line across one side and across the other edge. Mark the midpoint of the line on each edge; this is where you will begin drilling in step 2.

2. (See Figure 7-7.) To minimize friction, the hole through the body for the arms is drilled larger than the axle (dowel) diameter. Each end is then plugged with a dowel, which is then drilled slightly larger than the diameter of the axle. Since it is almost impossible to drill a hole accurately through a block of wood this

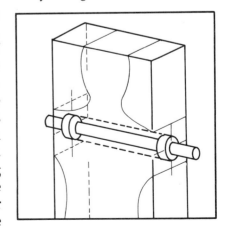

FIG. 7-7. *Axle holes for the arms.*

wide (without a drill press), you will be drilling the axle hole from each side.

Begin by drilling perpendicular pilot holes in each edge with a ³⁄₃₂″ bit to a depth of about 2″. Then redrill each edge with a ⁵⁄₁₆″ bit to a depth slightly greater than half the width of the body. If the holes are properly aligned, the bit should pass through the opening. If it doesn't, redrill from both directions, angling the bit as necessary to open the passage through the block. Be careful that you don't open the ends of the hole more than ⁵⁄₁₆″, as the ⁵⁄₁₆″ dowel plugs, which will be inserted next, must fit snugly in each end.

3. Cut the ⁵⁄₁₆″ dowel into two ¼″ lengths. Lightly cover the sides of each dowel with wood glue and carefully push one into each ⁵⁄₁₆″ hole on the edge of the block until they are flush with the edge; gently tap with a hammer if necessary. Allow the glue to dry thoroughly (½ hour). Mark the center of each dowel, establish a pilot hole by drilling with a ³⁄₃₂″ bit, then redrill with a ¹³⁄₆₄″ bit. Check the alignment of these holes by inserting a ³⁄₁₆″ dowel through the block. "Open" (redrill with a slight rotation of the bit) each hole as needed to allow free movement of the dowel. Remove the dowel and set it aside.

4. The hat will be attached to the top of the head later with a glued dowel peg. For the exact placement of the hat, go ahead and mark the center of the top edge of the block and drill a perpendicular hole to a depth of about ½″ with a ³⁄₁₆″ bit.

5. Now cut along the body outline with a saber, band, or coping saw.

MAKING THE ARMS AND FLAG PADDLES

1. Transfer the arm pattern (page 132) to the 1″ x 4″ pine, placing the straight side of the pattern along the planed edge of the wood. Be certain that the grain runs parallel to the length of the arm. Using a square, extend the top and bottom shoulder lines of the pattern across the edge. Mark the center between these lines (for the axle holes). Repeat for the other arm.

2. For ease of handling, clamp each arm to a flat surface. It's critical that each hole be drilled exactly perpendicular to the edge — the slightest variation will cause a wobbly arm rotation. To make sure it is perpendicular, each ⁵⁄₈″-deep hole will be drilled with a ³⁄₁₆″ bit in three increments: drill ¼″, another ¼″, then the final ⅛″. After each step, remove the drill and insert the uncut length of ³⁄₁₆″ dowel into the hole. Note the position of the dowel. If you are drilling correctly, the dowel will stand straight up; if it leans, adjust the angle of the drill slightly. When you have drilled a hole in each arm, cut a 5″ length of ³⁄₁₆″ dowel for the axle.

3. Now cut out the arms, using a saber, band, or coping saw.

4. Trace the flag paddle pattern onto ³⁄₃₂″ basswood and use a fine-tooth saw blade to cut them out. (If you can't find basswood, use any thin wood.) Thin wood is fragile, so sand the edges gently with a fine-grit paper.

5. Study the drawings of the arm in Figure 7-8 to understand the location and angle of the paddle slots. Draw a slot *slightly* less than the thickness of the paddle across the end of one hand at a 45-degree angle. With the arm clamped, cut the slot to a depth of ⅜″. Now mark and cut the other arm, using the *exact* same angle and depth. A paddle should fit snugly into each slot.

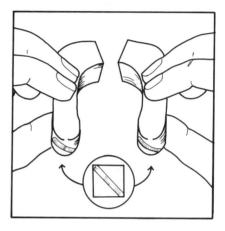

FIG. 7-8. *Cut the paddle slots at a 45-degree angle.*

MAKING THE HAT AND SHOES

1. Transfer the hat brim pattern to a piece of ³⁄₃₂″ basswood and cut it out. The 1⅝″ length of 1⅛″ dowel is for the top of the hat. Find the exact center of each and mark them accordingly. Drill through the center of the brim, using a ³⁄₁₆″ bit; then with the same bit, drill into the center of the top of the hat to a depth of about ½″. Cut a 1″ length of ³⁄₁₆″ dowel and set it aside; the hat will be completed at the end of the project.

2. Transfer the shoe pattern (the grain should be running from the top to the bottom of the shoe) to 1″ pine and cut; repeat for the other shoe.

3. Cut two 1¾″ pieces of ³⁄₁₆″ dowel for attaching the shoes to the legs, and cut two 1½″ pieces of ³⁄₁₆″ dowel for attaching the shoes to the base.

(Text continues on page 133.)

Uncle Sam Whirligig Wood Patterns

BODY

Cut 1 from 5/4″ x 4″ x 11″ pine

Centerline indicates drill guideline at top of head for hat dowel.

NOTE: For a taller Uncle Sam, add ½″ to legs.

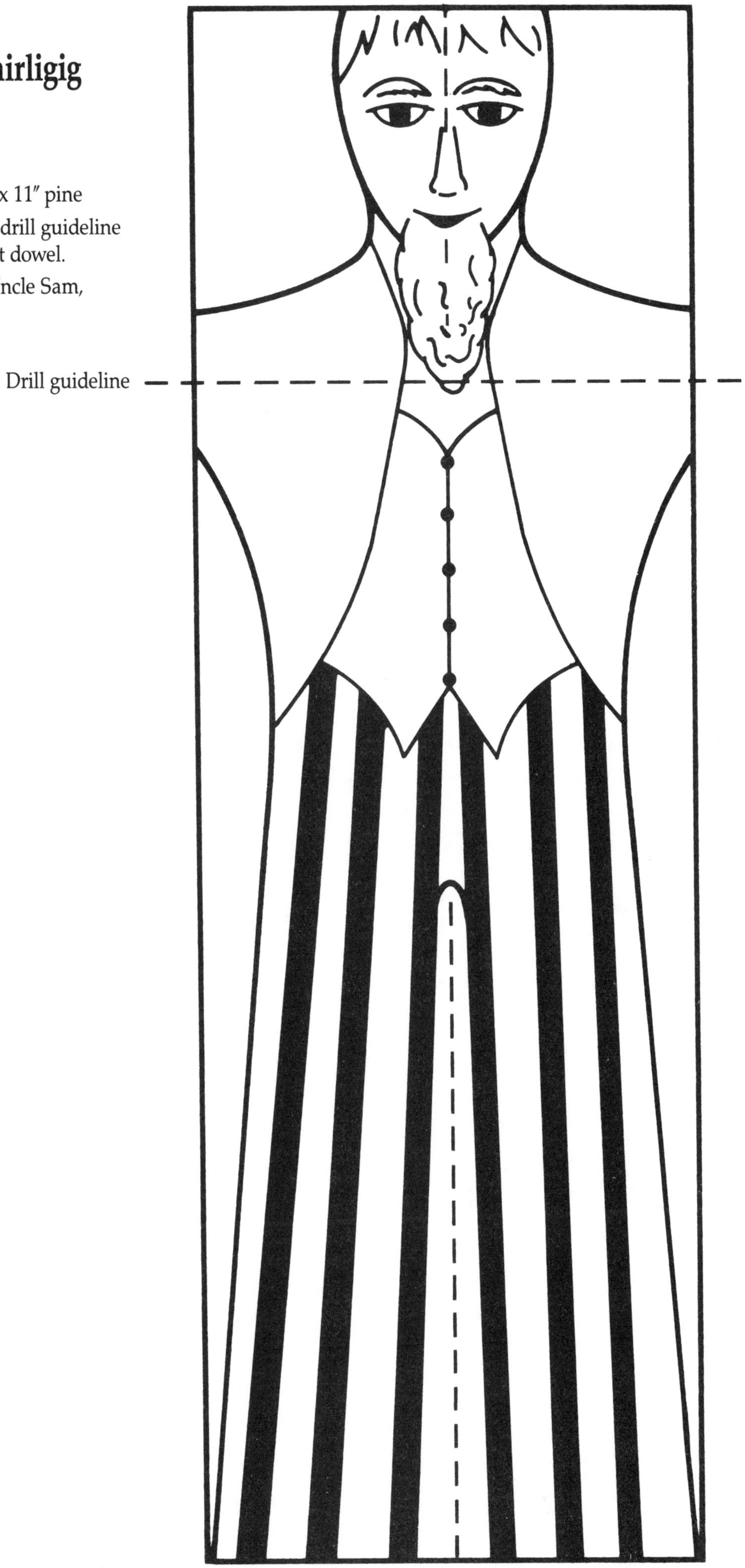

Drill guideline — — — —

Uncle Sam Whirligig Wood Patterns (continued)

ARM
Cut 2 from 1″ pine

Drill
guideline

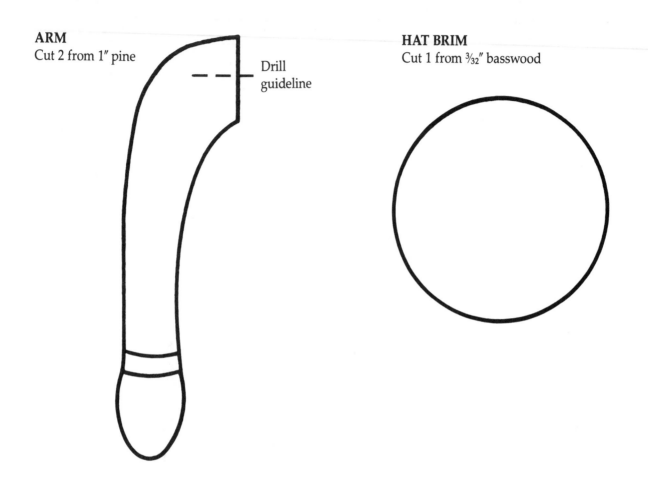

HAT BRIM
Cut 1 from ³⁄₃₂″ basswood

FLAG PADDLE
Cut 2 from ³⁄₃₂″ basswood

SHOE
Cut 2 from 1″ pine

CARVING THE WHIRLIGIG

NOTE: Clothing details (with the exception of the collar at the neckline) are painted rather than carved.

1. Using short controlled cuts, round the face and head. *Do not* round the top of the head; it must remain level to accommodate the hat. Don't try to carve a completely round head; it will remain somewhat flat in the front and back because of the thickness of the wood. The eyebrows, nose, and beard will be carved in bas-relief. Simply stated, you will be removing the wood surrounding the lines: that is, the cheeks and mouth area, the forehead, and the area surrounding the beard. With the point of your knife, first cut straight down about ⅛" to outline the pattern lines. Then, using tiny strokes, carefully shave away the surrounding wood. (See Figure 7-9.) Dig the mouth out slightly with the tip of your blade. For a more pronounced nose, you can glue a separate small piece of wood onto the face and then shape it. You may also want to carve a bas-relief collar at the back of the neck.

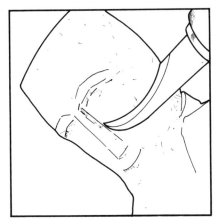

Fig. 7-9. *Carve the eyebrows, nose, and beard in bas-relief.*

2. Use the straight cut to carefully remove all sharp edges on the body. Using the paring or thumb-assist stroke, round and shape the shoulders and waist. Carve the chest slightly around the beard (to make the beard more pronounced). Carve the legs into an almost cylindrical shape. Work slowly; you can always remove more wood, but it's impossible to put removed wood back in place. Use the V-cut for removing wood in the tight spots between the legs.

3. Shape and round the edges of the shoes.

4. Shape and round the arms and hands. To rotate properly, the arms must be of equal size and weight, so work slowly, turning and comparing the shape as you carve. To minimize friction inside the body, wax the parts of the axle that will contact the armhole plug. Insert the axle through the body and attach the arms. Place the arms in exact opposite positions — one up, the other down. If the arms are well balanced, they will remain in any position in which they are placed; if not, the lighter one will rise. Trim the heavier one until they are balanced. (If you overdrilled the armholes, causing the axle to slip inside the arm, build up the circumference of the dowel by spreading a thin coat of glue on the end of the dowel and dipping it in fine sawdust. Let it dry thoroughly.) Once the arms are properly balanced, remove them and set them aside.

5. Smooth all parts, using either sandpaper or the edge of your knife. Wipe with a tack cloth.

PAINTING THE WHIRLIGIG

1. Since the finished carved body is considerably smaller than the actual pattern, the clothing lines on the pattern serve only as a guide; the clothing must be drawn on the body freehand to suit the finished size of your whirligig. Referring to the pattern and the back view of the body on page 134, lightly pencil the clothing lines on the front and back of the body. Do not draw the stripes on the pants because they would be covered when you paint the base coat.

2. Paint the vest with Honey Comb and, before it dries, mix a small amount of Coffee Bean with Honey Comb on your palette and shade along the edge of the vest (where it meets the coat) and down the center. Paint the buttons with Coffee Bean (try painting small dots such as these buttons by dipping the handle end of a small paintbrush into the paint, then dabbing it on the vest for each button). Paint the pants and the top three quarters of the hat with Taffy; when dry, pencil in the stripes and paint them using Red Clay thinned with extender (so the paint will flow more easily). Paint the jacket, sleeves, brim of the hat, and band around the bottom of the hat with Paisley Blue (for an aged and weathered look, add a small amount of Wrought Iron to the blue and thin it slightly with water). Paint the shirt, cuffs, and stars on the hat white, and the shoes Wrought Iron.

3. Paint the face and hands Apricot Cream. Using the dry-brush technique (see Glossary, page 157), add a blush to the cheeks with Red Clay. Paint the hair, brows, and beard white. Paint the mouth Red Clay and the eyes white with Coffee Bean irises. Highlight each eye with a tiny fleck of white.

(Text continues on page 135.)

Uncle Sam Whirligig
Painting Guides

BODY — Back View

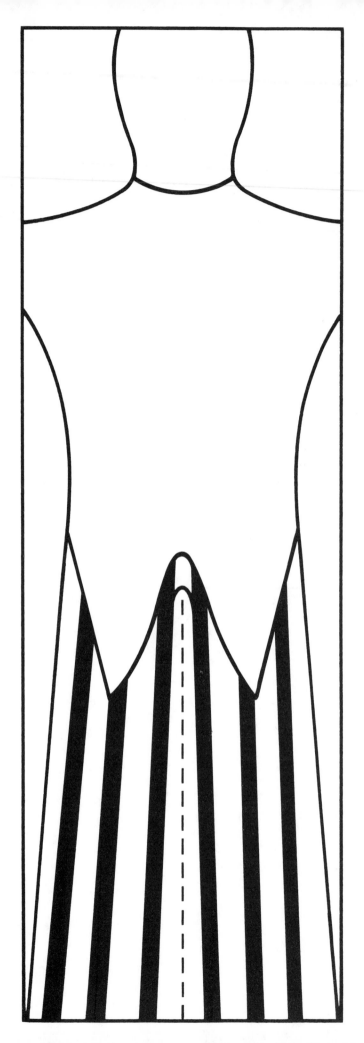

TOP OF HAT

4. Paint the flag paddles with red and white stripes, a blue background with white stars at the handle end (use the pattern as a guide).

5. Stain or paint the base black.

6. Antique, if desired, using the techniques described in Chapter 1, page 20.

PUTTING IT TOGETHER

1. Glue and insert the 1″ length of ³⁄₁₆″ dowel into the ½″ hole drilled in the top of the head. Press the hat brim and then the top of the hat onto the dowel. Rotate, if necessary, for the best angle. When the hat is level on the head, spread a thin layer of glue between all three pieces and press in place. If the hat is not level, redrill the hole or whittle the dowel to achieve an even fit. When it is level, glue it in place.

2. Hold the body upside down, resting the top of the hat on a flat surface. Position one shoe on a leg and, using a ³⁄₁₆″ bit, drill through the center of the shoe and about ½″ into the leg. It is important to hold the shoe firmly while drilling the hole; if it shifts, the shoe will not be level with the leg. Cover a 1¾″ length of ³⁄₁₆″ dowel with wood glue, and with a hammer, gently drive the glued dowel all the way into the hole. With a coping saw, cut the dowel flush with the bottom of the shoe. Repeat to attach the other shoe.

3. Center the whirligig on the base and trace the outline of the shoes on the top of the base. Remove the whirligig and set the base on a piece of scrap wood about the size of the base (to prevent the base from splintering as the drill bit comes out the other side). With a ³⁄₁₆″ bit, drill through the top of the base at the center of each shoe tracing. To open the holes completely, redrill from the other side.

Lightly coat the bottom of each shoe with glue, position the whirligig on the traced shoe outlines, and, without allowing any movement of the base, stand the whirligig upside down. Now place the ³⁄₁₆″ bit into one of the holes in the bottom of the base and, using the hole as a guide, drill into the shoe to a depth of no more than ½″. Tap the shavings out of the hole and insert a glued 1½″ length of ³⁄₁₆″ dowel. Repeat for the other shoe.

4. Glue and insert one end of the axle into an arm, place a washer on the axle, and push the axle through the body. Then put a washer on the other side and place the remaining arm in the opposite position. Check the length of the axle; if it is too long (you should have no more than ¹⁄₁₆″ play along the axle), cut it to fit. When you are satisfied with the fit, apply glue to the axle and attach the arm permanently. To ensure a balanced spin, quickly position the arms in exactly opposite directions before the glue dries.

5. Glue the flags into the hand slots. Spin the arms before the glue sets to be certain that the flags clear the legs.

Lesser Yellowlegs Decoy

SUPPLIES

2″ x 4″ x 10″ block of basswood or 2″ x 6″ x 9″ block of pine

3½″ length of 2″ x 4″ pine or 3″ length of 3″-wide tree branch for a base

9½″ length of ¼″ dowel

Tracing and graphite paper, pencil, ruler, masking tape

Saber, band, or coping saw

Drill with ¼″ bit

Wood glue

X-acto knife or jackknife

Sandpaper (medium and fine)

Tack cloth

Stain (optional)

Clear nail polish or satin-finish clear varnish

Sealer (optional)

Acrylic paint (Folk Art colors: Taffy, black, Red Clay)

No. 2 round brush, No. 2 and No. 8 natural-bristle flat brushes, 1″ sponge brush

Paper plate, paper towels

Stylus or toothpick

Two ¼″ glass or plastic eyes (optional)

DECOYS — artificial birds made to lure live birds within a hunter's range — are an American invention. This method of hunting was developed by the Indians, whose decoys were fashioned from piles of mud, bundles of grass, or stuffed skins. Their methods were later adopted and then refined by early New England settlers.

Although styles differed according to the period and region of the maker, basically two types of decoys were made: floaters and stick-ups. Floaters, used on the water to lure waterfowl such as swans, geese, and ducks, were often made from two carved and hollowed-out wood pieces joined in the center. Stick-ups, made of wood or tin, were attached to a stick, then stuck in the sand or marshy bay areas to attract land-loving shore birds such as snipes, sandpipers, and curlews. Some stick-ups were simply flat, two-dimensional silhouettes known as "flatties"; others were carved in the round from a solid block of wood, then primitively painted. Since most early decoys were considered nothing more than tools to harvest a crop, little time was spent painting or carving fine details, and they often bore only a slight resemblance to the wildfowl they were designed to attract.

During the late nineteenth and early twentieth centuries, as hunting increased and the number of birds declined, decoy makers began to fashion better and more detailed decoys in hopes of attracting the dwindling number of birds. One of the best known decoy artists from this period was Elmer Crowell, whose beautifully carved and painted birds are avidly sought by folk art collectors today. Decoys are still made and used for hunting certain species of wildfowl, but many are so exquisitely crafted that they will never see water and are meant to lure only flocks of collectors.

The lesser yellowlegs decoy makes a handsome addition to a bookshelf, mantel, or windowsill. For a fuller-bodied decoy, start with a 2″ or thicker block of basswood; for a slightly flat-sided version, you can substitute a 2″-thick block of pine (planed thickness will be 1½″). The No. 8 flat brush in the supply list is needed for the feathering technique and should be worn, with slightly splayed bristles, to work properly. You can either paint the eyes on the bird or buy glass or plastic ones at a hobby shop.

Detail from color plate 4.

MAKING THE DECOY

1. Transfer the side-view pattern (page 138) of the bird to the side of the block; make certain that the grain of the wood runs from head to tail. Using a saber, band, or coping saw, cut along the outside of the pattern lines to remove the excess wood. (See Figure 7-10.)

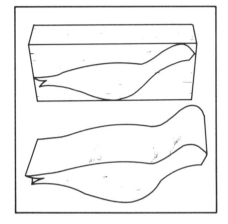

FIG. 7-10. *Cut away the excess wood outside the pattern lines.*

2. Draw a line down the center of the top and bottom of the block, then sketch or transfer the top-view pattern to the top (adjust the width of the pattern to the thickness of your block). (See Figure 7-11.) Saw along the pattern lines to remove excess wood from the head, neck, and tail areas. (See Figure 7-12.)

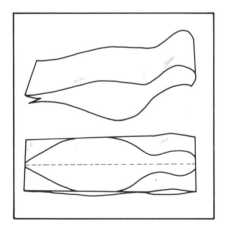

FIG. 7-11. *Transfer the top-view pattern to the top of the block.*

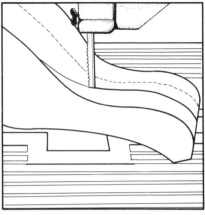

FIG. 7-12. *Cut away the excess wood from the head, neck, and tail.*

3. Mark the positions of the beak and leg (see the side-view pattern) and, using a ¼" bit, drill into the wood about ¾" at each mark. Be careful of the position of the bit while drilling; you don't want the beak or leg to be inserted at the wrong angle.

4. Using a ¼" bit, drill into the center of the base to a depth of about ¾".

5. Cut a 6¼" length of dowel for the leg, leaving a 3¼" piece for the beak. Glue the beak in place before shaping it. (Shaping and painting the beak will come later and will be easier once the beak is in place and supported by the bird.)

CARVING THE DECOY

1. Round the edges and do any preliminary shaping with the straight cut. Work slowly, removing only a little wood at a time; remember always to carve with the grain.

2. Starting at the neck and working down, begin rounding the body of the bird, using well-controlled small strokes (paring or thumb-assist). Always work back and forth, from one side to the other, comparing the sides as you go and using the center pencil lines as guides for keeping the sides symmetrical. (Refer to Figure 7-13 for general body shape.) Work slowly and carefully so you won't overcarve a section.

(Text continues on page 139.)

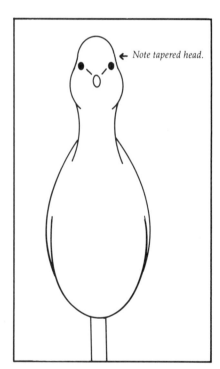

FIG. 7-13. *The shape of the decoy, front view.*

Lesser Yellowlegs Decoy Wood Patterns

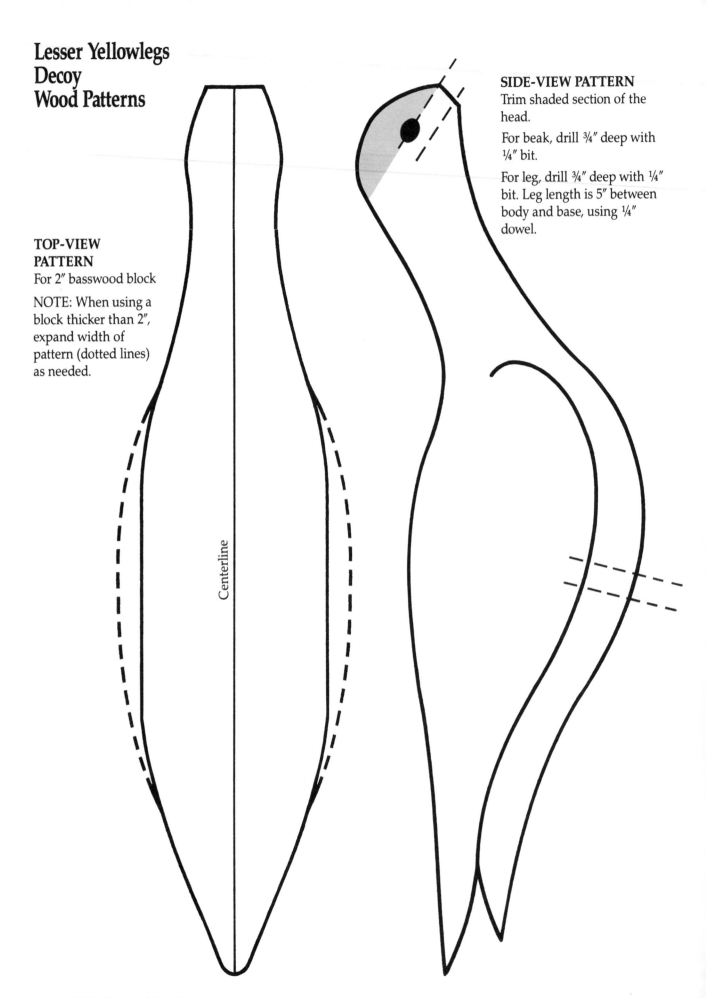

TOP-VIEW PATTERN
For 2″ basswood block

NOTE: When using a block thicker than 2″, expand width of pattern (dotted lines) as needed.

Centerline

SIDE-VIEW PATTERN
Trim shaded section of the head.

For beak, drill ¾″ deep with ¼″ bit.

For leg, drill ¾″ deep with ¼″ bit. Leg length is 5″ between body and base, using ¼″ dowel.

3. If you are carving on the full 2″-thick block, draw the outline of the wings on the body with a pencil. (See the side-view pattern.) With the tip of your knife, cut down to a depth of about ⅛″ along this line. Now, using a shallow shaving motion, carve out the area under the wings, working toward the tail. (See Figure 7-14.) You will have to go over this area several times to get enough depth to define the wings. Taper the wing tips.

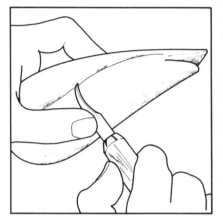

FIG. 7-14. *Carving the wings.*

If you have chosen to use a 2″ pine block (1½″ planed), paint rather than carve the wings; the wood is not thick enough for you to define the wings by carving. Round and shape the underside of the body.

4. A bird's head is wider at the bottom than at the top. Using Figure 7-13 and the shaded section on the side-view pattern as guides, carefully taper and round the head.

5. Using Figure 7-15 as a guide, begin carving the beak. Slowly shave away the wood (thumb-assist stroke), trimming and tapering all sides to a finished length of about 2⅛″ to 2¼″. Sand until smooth.

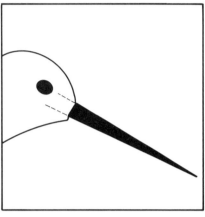

FIG. 7-15. *The decoy's beak.*

6. Starting with medium-grit sandpaper, sand the body, removing all whittle marks. Sand gently around the carved wing area with fine-grit paper. Finish by sanding the body smooth with fine-grit paper.

FINISHING

For a simple yet attractive alternative to painting, stain the decoy, allowing the natural beauty of the wood to show through. After sanding, wipe the decoy with a tack cloth and apply the stain of your choice. Let it dry, then apply a coat of clear varnish. Note that the beak (dowel) might not stain the same shade as the bird.

To free your hands while painting, use the leg dowel and base as a pedestal (cover the top inch of the dowel with masking tape to protect it from paint spatters). A dry-brush technique called feathering can be used to simulate markings and feathers. Feathering is done by dipping a well-worn bristle brush (one on which the bristles have become slightly separated) into your paint, then stroking the brush across a paper towel until much of the paint is removed. It's important that your brush be almost dry. Then, using a very light, wispy touch and a sweeping motion of the wrist, apply the paint. Refer to Figure 7-16 and color plate 4 while painting.

1. Seal the wood, if desired, let dry, then sand lightly. Wipe with a tack cloth.

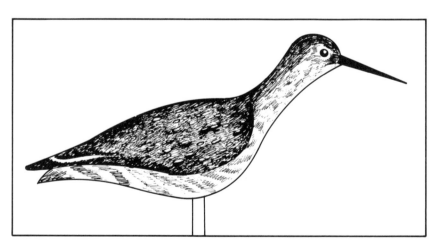

FIG. 7-16. *Painting guide for the decoy.*

2. Using a 1" sponge brush, base-coat the entire body with Taffy. While the paint is still wet, brush black on the wings and back with the No. 8 flat brush, blending the colors as you go to get a soft gray color. For a feathery look, allow bits of the base color to show through.

3. Mix Taffy and black on a paper plate to get a medium gray color. Using the worn bristle brush, feather the markings on the tail, along the neck and head, and under the wings.

4. Using the No. 2 flat brush dipped in black, paint the beak. Then using the No. 8 flat brush dipped in black, lightly outline the wings and paint the detail lines on the wing tips and the markings around the eyes. Dry-brush the feathers along the back, neck, head, and wings with black. Add a few dark markings under the wings.

5. Paint the feather detail on the wing tips with Taffy, then dry-brush some feathers along the back and sides. With a stylus or toothpick dipped in Taffy, apply dots randomly on the back and wings.

6. If you plan to paint the eyes, paint them with Red Clay. Allow them to dry, then paint large black pupils. Highlight each eye with a tiny fleck of Taffy. When dry, add a gloss by applying a bead of clear nail polish or varnish over each eye.

If you plan to use glass or plastic eyes, drill or carve eye sockets to match the size of the eyes. Apply a small amount of glue to each hole, then press the eyes into place.

7. Remove the masking tape from the end of the leg dowel. For a weathered look, mix Taffy with black to make a light gray and add water to make a wash. Paint or stain the leg. When dry, apply glue to each end and push one end into the decoy and the other into the base.

8. Antique the decoy if you wish by lightly rubbing the body with fine-grit sandpaper. Not only does this make the decoy look older, but when done on the dark wing areas, it also creates a more feathery, lifelike appearance. If desired, finish with a burnt umber glaze, Chapter 1, page 20.

8
Country
Furniture

NOTHING SUGGESTS country in a room more effectively than the clean, simple lines of a beautifully handcrafted piece of antique pine furniture. Most aficionados of country decorating, however, have experienced the disappointment of ferreting out that perfect find in a shop or at a country auction, only to have to pass it by upon discovering the price. But don't be dismayed; you can still create that special look and homespun feeling by making the beautiful country-style pieces in this chapter. Although they possess the simple lines and functional utility so characteristic of their antique counterparts, the method of construction has been simplified, enabling anyone with the desire and some basic woodworking tools and skills to make a roomful of charming furniture on a shoestring budget.

Many early pieces of country furniture were either painted or grain-painted (a technique used to simulate the look of high-style woods such as rosewood and mahogany) to hide the natural grain of the less-than-desirable pine. This is not the case today. Antique pine furniture, with its natural woody warmth and down-home appeal, is a highly sought-after collectible. You can either stain these pieces, if you wish to accent the mellow tone and natural grain of the wood, or paint them. For an aged, weathered appearance, paint the piece with an acrylic wash, made by diluting the paint with water until it is almost translucent. Many of the old pieces were painted with milk paint, so you might consider using that for a really authentic look. (See Chapter 1, page 11, for both.) I have given some suggestions, but since finishing is a matter of taste and decor, that final touch will be up to you.

The projects in this chapter are presented according to the level of skill needed. If you are new to woodworking or if your skills have become a little rusty, review the information given in Chapter 1. Start with a simple project such as the child's settle bench, and once you've gained some confidence, progress to the others. Whether your style is country or contemporary, any one of these pieces is sure to find a place in your home. They may not be antiques, but for the pride you'll feel when you've finished one, they might as well be!

All the projects are made from standard-size No. 2 pine, and whenever possible, to save cutting time, the instructions give the pre-planed measurements of the store-bought lumber, except for length, which is always the *actual* measurement. (Beware of warpage when choosing lumber for these projects; it can make for less satisfactory results.) When you are marking each piece of wood for cutting, picture its appearance as part of the finished piece. Try to use pieces with an attractive grain in places where the grain will be seen. Avoid layout measurements that will place knots on cutting lines or at points where the piece will be nailed or screwed. To allow for defects, the lengths of wood given in the supply lists are sometimes greater than the amount you will actually use.

A universal symbol of love and a commonly used folk art motif, the heart appears in one form or another with cheerful regularity on these pieces. Cut-out designs such as the heart can be made with a saber saw in one of two ways. One method is to drill a ⅜" hole anywhere within the area to be cut out and then insert the saw blade through the drill hole to begin the cut. The second method is to turn the saber saw on end, with the front of the saw plate (the shoe) resting on the wood and the blade parallel to and directly over (but *not touching*) the area to be removed. Holding the saw firmly, turn it on and *slowly* lower the blade into the wood, pivoting the saw downward. When the blade is through the wood, cut out the design with the saw plate resting on the wood as usual. This step is optional, however; if desired, stencil a design in place of the cut-out heart or leave that part of the piece unadorned.

Child's Settle Bench

FEW pieces can be as easily reproduced as this charming, straight-backed child's settle bench, styled after those so common in American homes from the late seventeenth through the eighteenth century. Since homes of that era had no central heating, the high, slightly enclosed back of the settle served to shield a person from drafts in a cold room. Because this bench takes only a few dollars and a couple of hours to make, it is the ideal project for the novice woodworker. Why not surprise your little ones with their very own "no adults allowed" bench? No small children at home? Make it anyway — it's the perfect size for displaying a collection of your favorite dolls or teddies!

Since this design does not have a cut-out heart, as do the other pieces in this chapter, stencil a design instead (the pattern is included). The bench pictured below was antiqued by gently sanding the flat surfaces and edges to simulate wear. The faded, dusty color of the milk paint, combined with the gentle sanding, gives it a look of such authentic wear that most people are surprised to learn it's not an antique.

SUPPLIES
Two 1" x 12" x 48" pieces of No. 2 pine
12" piece of scrap lumber
28" x 44" piece of poster board,
    yardstick, pencil, scissors
Saber saw
Rasp or plane
Square
C-clamp
Tape measure
Sandpaper (medium and fine)
Twelve 8d finishing nails, hammer
Wood filler
Paint or stain
6½" x 8½" sheet of Mylar, X-acto knife,
    pane of glass, masking tape for
    stenciling (optional)

LAYING OUT AND CUTTING THE PIECES
(Refer to Figure 8-1)

1. Enlarge the side-piece pattern on page 144 to scale; transfer the seat and nail placement points to the pattern.

2. Both side pieces (A) will be cut from the same board. It is important that no knots be located on any cut lines or on the seat placement line, so choose the clearer of the two boards for these pieces. Trace the enlarged pattern onto the board, keeping the straight side of the pattern along the edge of the board. Transfer the seat placement line (*a* to *b*) and the nail placement marks (*c*, *d*, and *e*) by pushing a nail or sharp pencil point through the pattern to the wood. Turn the pattern over and repeat for

Detail from color plate 7.

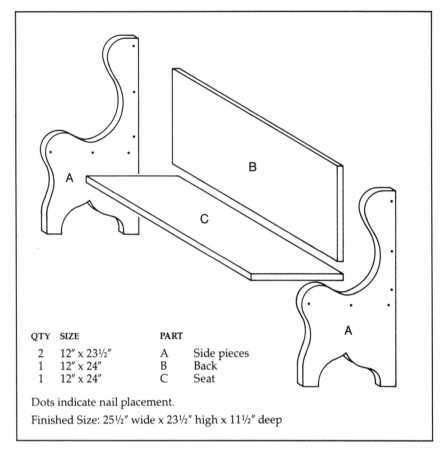

QTY	SIZE		PART	
2	12″ x 23½″		A	Side pieces
1	12″ x 24″		B	Back
1	12″ x 24″		C	Seat

Dots indicate nail placement.

Finished Size: 25½″ wide x 23½″ high x 11½″ deep

FIG. 8-1. *Child's settle bench assembly.*

the other side piece. Cut out both pieces, then draw the seat placement line on one side of each so that it will be on the inside of the bench. Round the cut edges with a rasp or plane.

3. Divide the length of the remaining board in half with a light pencil line (use a framing square to ensure right angles). One half will be the back (B), the other the seat (C); each piece will be 24″ long. Support both ends while cutting to avoid splitting as you near the end of the cut. With a rasp or plane, round one edge only of each piece; rasp or plane the cut ends as needed to ensure square, even cuts. Sand the pieces.

PUTTING IT TOGETHER

1. Since it would be impossible to hold the nails and hold the pieces together while joining them, it is necessary to drive the nails *just* through the side piece (the nail points should be barely visible on the other side) before you assemble the pieces. Before you begin, place a 12″ length of scrap lumber under the side piece at the seat placement line; this will prevent you from driving the nails into your work surface.

Start one 8d nail at each nail placement mark. Repeat on the other side piece. Place one end of the seat piece on the floor; while holding it upright, position a side piece on the other end. Align the upper end of the seat on the seat placement mark (on the side piece); the back edges of both pieces should be flush, the rounded edge to the front. Drive in the nails. Turn the bench over and attach the other side piece in the same way.

2. With the bench resting on one end, place the back piece between the side pieces, resting the edge on the seat. Drive three evenly spaced nails through each side piece into the back. Countersink the nail heads ⅛″ (see Chapter 1, page 19) and fill the holes with wood filler. Sand them flush when dry.

3. Paint or stain the bench. To reproduce the heart design along the upper edge of the back, position the stencil to one side of center, tape it in place, and stencil. Then turn it over and repeat on the other side to complete the design. If you want to antique the bench, refer to Chapter 1, page 20, for instructions.

Child's Settle Bench Wood Pattern for Side Pieces

Points *a* to *b* — seat placement line
Points *c, d,* and *e* — nail placement marks
One square equals 1″

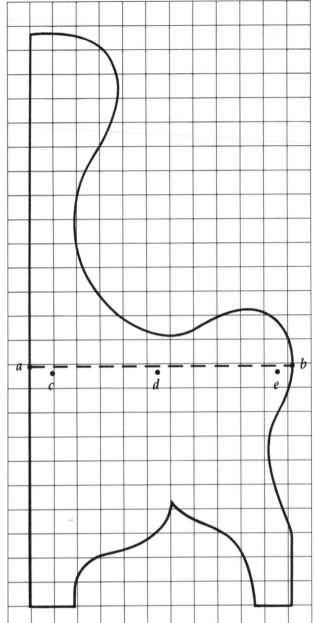

Child's Settle Bench Stencil Pattern

Cut 1 stencil; reverse to stencil other side.

Centerline

Quilt Rack

T HE classic lines of this simple quilt rack will add instant country warmth to any room in your home, so don't restrict it to the bedroom; it's perfect for displaying a cherished heirloom quilt in a living room or family room, or a collection of pretty guest towels in your bath; or bring it into the kitchen to hang-dry bunches of herbs and flowers. On a more practical note, use it to store blankets and coverlets during those in-between months when it can be chilly one night and warm the next. Now that you've realized you just can't be without one, give it a try!

The design that follows, like the others in this chapter, uses standard sizes of commonly found lumber, making this another quick, easy, and satisfying project.

SUPPLIES
Two 1″ x 10″ x 48″ pieces of No. 2 pine
One 1⅛″ x 8′ round fir pole (dowel)
One 1″ x 3″ x 48″ piece of No. 2 pine
Tape measure or yardstick, pencil
Square
Saber saw
Tracing and graphite paper, tape
1-gallon and 1-quart paint cans
Rasp or plane
Sandpaper (medium and fine), tack cloth
Drill with 1⅛″ spade bit and No. 10 screw counterbore bit
Miter box (optional)
Ten 2″ No. 10 flat-head wood screws, flat-tipped screwdriver
Ten ⁵⁄₁₆″ round-top wooden buttons, hammer, wood glue
Paint or stain
C-clamp (optional)

LAYING OUT AND CUTTING THE PATTERN
(Refer to Figure 8-2, page 147)

1. To make the side pieces (A), measure and mark a 32″ length on each 1″ x 10″ x 48″ board. Avoid having any knots where there will be cuts or screw holes. Square both ends and cut. Divide the width of the board in half and, with a lightly drawn pencil line, mark a centerline from top to bottom. (The pencil-marked sides will be on the inside of the quilt rack when it is assembled.)

2. Transfer the half pattern for the legs (page 146) to one end of the board; turn the pattern over to complete the other half of the design. Repeat on the other side piece.

(Text continues on page 147.)

Detail from color plate 7.

Quilt Rack Half Pattern
for Bottom of Side Panel

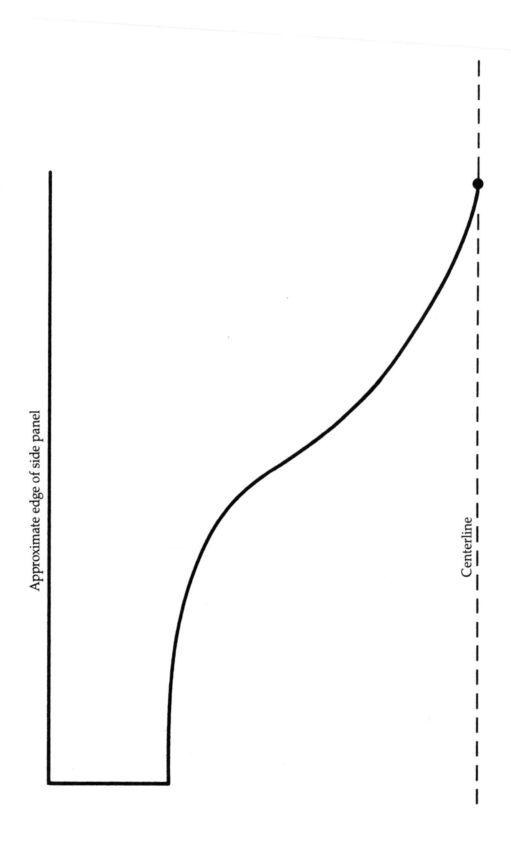

Approximate edge of side panel

Centerline

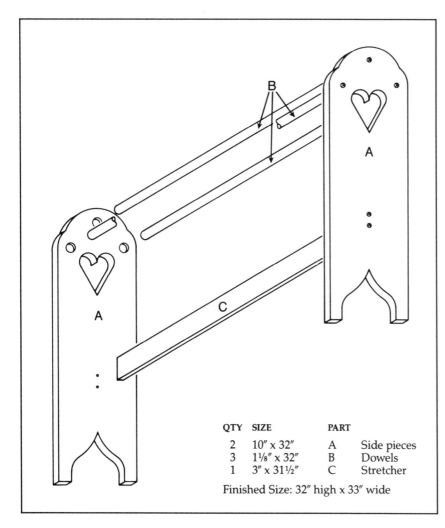

FIG. 8-2. *Quilt rack assembly.*

QTY	SIZE	PART	
2	10″ x 32″	A	Side pieces
3	1⅛″ x 32″	B	Dowels
1	3″ x 31½″	C	Stretcher

Finished Size: 32″ high x 33″ wide

3. A 1-gallon and a 1-quart paint can will be used to draw the scallops. (See Figure 8-3.) Place a mark 4½″ from the top edge of a side piece, and, using a square, draw a light pencil line across the board (*a*). To draw the first arc, center the gallon paint can on the centerline, with the edge of the can even with the top of the board; trace around the top half of the can to form a semicircle (line *b*) on line *a*. Center the quart can on line *a*, with the edge of the can even with one side of the board; trace from the edge of the board to line *b* (solid line *c*). Repeat on the other side of the board. Then repeat all steps on the remaining side piece.

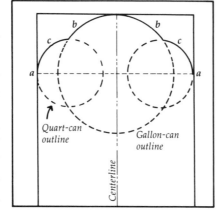

FIG. 8-3. *Guide for drawing the scallops.*

4. Cut out the legs and the scallops. If desired, round the edges of the side pieces with a rasp or a plane. Sand each side thoroughly, taking care not to remove the pencil centerline.

5. Place a mark on the centerline of each side piece, 1½″ from the top. Place marks on line *a* 1½″ from each edge. Drill each of these points to a depth of precisely ¼″ using a 1⅛″ spade bit. (To drill exactly ¼″, place a piece of masking tape all around the wide portion of the bit, leaving the point and ¼″ of the bit exposed.) These recesses are the seating holes for the dowels. Note that the point of the spade bit will come through the other side of the board, thereby providing the location for the screw holes to be drilled in a later step.

6. Measure down the centerline from the top and place a mark at 10″. Place the bottom point of the heart pattern (page 148) on this mark and center the pattern on the centerline. Trace the pattern and cut it out with a saber-saw. Repeat on the other side piece.

7. Again measure down the centerline from the top and mark in four places: 19½″, 20½″, 21¼″, and 21¾″. At the 19½″ and 21¾″ marks, use a square to extend each of these marks about 1″ on both sides of the centerline; these marks will help in positioning the stretcher while it is being screwed in place. Using a No. 10 counterbore bit with the ⅛″ drill bit portion extended at least ¾″, carefully drill through the board at the other two marks (20½″ and 21¼″). Be sure that the holes are perpendicular to the board and that they are *not* countersunk. Repeat on the other side piece.

8. Turn the board over and counterbore all five stretcher and dowel holes to a depth of approximately 3/16″. Do *not* counterbore too deeply, especially the top three holes; you must leave enough of the board intact to hold the screw heads. Repeat on the other side piece.

9. Cut the 1⅛" dowel into three 32" lengths. Hold a dowel piece with one end resting on the floor and, using the counterbore bit (with the drill bit portion extended at least ¾"), drill a centered hole in the other end to a depth of about ¾". Turn the dowel around and drill the other end. Repeat with the other two dowel pieces.

10. Cut a 31½" length of 1" x 3" pine for the stretcher and sand it. For a proper fit, both ends must be square; a miter box is helpful in ensuring this.

PUTTING IT TOGETHER

1. With one end of a dowel resting on the floor, place the other end in a hole in one of the side pieces. Install a screw through the side piece and into the dowel. Tighten to take up the slack, but be careful not to overtighten. Screw the other end of the dowel into the other side piece. Once again, do not overtighten; you need to be able to install the other dowels without prying the side pieces apart. Attach the other two dowels in the same manner.

2. Using the pencil lines drawn across the centerline to help position it, hold the stretcher in place and install two screws through each side piece into the stretcher.

3. Tighten all screws.

4. Apply a small amount of glue to each round-top wooden button. Gently tap one into place in each counterbored screw hole.

5. Wipe all parts with a tack cloth, then paint or stain. If you choose to stain, be aware that since the dowels are fir and orangish in color and all other pieces are pine, the dowels will stain a slightly different shade. You can compensate for this by first staining the entire piece dark walnut and then staining all the pine pieces with colonial maple.

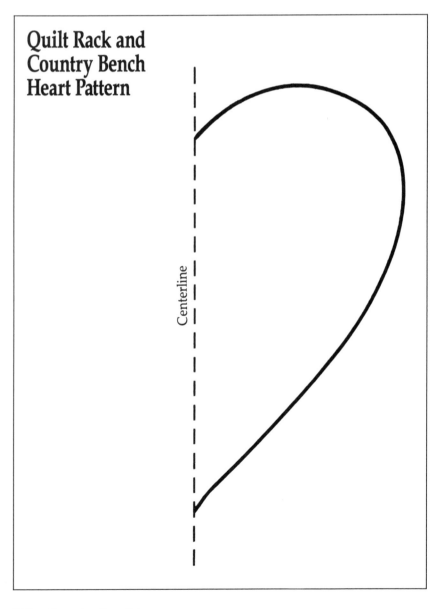

Quilt Rack and Country Bench Heart Pattern

Centerline

Country Bench

THIS simple country bench is styled after those made more than a century and a half ago in rural villages all across the country. At that time, benches of this sort were as common in the home as they were at social gatherings and church suppers. While this double-apron bench is designed to be used with the trestle table (page 152), you'll undoubtedly find endless other uses and places for it. Until I had two, I found myself shuffling it from room to room, from indoors to out. It's perfect for placing on a porch, patio, or near your garden as a planter's bench. But don't go too far with it — you might need it for extra seating at a large holiday dinner or a child's birthday party. Whatever use you have in mind, you're sure to appreciate its durability, versatility, and ease of construction.

The instructions that follow are for a 48" bench. You can shorten or extend the length to suit your needs.

LAYING OUT AND CUTTING THE PIECES
(Refer to Figure 8-4)

1. Select a relatively knot-free 1" x 12" x 48" pine board for the seat (A) and set it aside.

2. The legs (B) are attached to the seat at an angle, making it necessary to cut both ends of each leg (and the stretcher in step 4) with your saw set at a 5-degree angle (Figure 8-5, page 150). (The angle of a saber saw blade can be easily changed by adjusting the shoe surrounding the blade.) The legs will be cut from the remaining 1" x 12" x 48" piece. To cut all four ends at the proper 5-degree angle, begin the first cut about 2" from the end of the board, measure from this point 17¾" and cut, then measure and cut the final 17¾" piece. Make all cuts from the same side of the board so that the angles will be parallel.

SUPPLIES
Two 1" x 12" x 48" pieces of pine
Two 1" x 6" x 48" pieces of pine
One 1" x 3" x 48" piece of pine
Tape measure, pencil
Saber saw
Square
Tracing and graphite paper
C-clamp
1-quart paint can or 1-pound coffee can
Sandpaper (medium and fine)
Twenty-eight 8d finishing nails, hammer
Wood filler
Rasp or plane
Nail set (optional)
Paint or stain

FIG. 8-4. *Country bench assembly.*

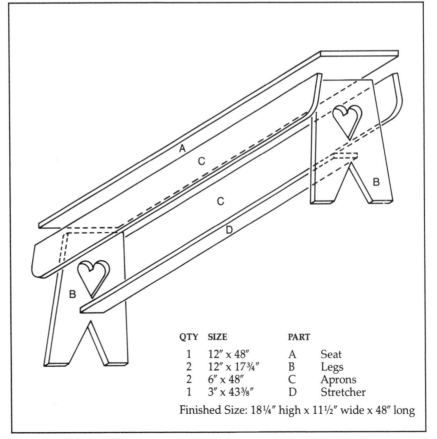

QTY	SIZE	PART	
1	12" x 48"	A	Seat
2	12" x 17¾"	B	Legs
2	6" x 48"	C	Aprons
1	3" x 43⅜"	D	Stretcher

Finished Size: 18¼" high x 11½" wide x 48" long

Detail from color plate 3.

After cutting, refer to Figure 8-5 to determine the inside and top end of each piece, according to the angles. All alignment and cut marks will be made on the inside of each leg piece. Draw a centerline from top to bottom on each piece (Figure 8-5, line *a*). At the top of each leg piece, measure in 1⅜″ from both edges and mark. Draw a straight line from each mark to the same-side corner at the bottom (Figure 8-5, lines *b*).

For the triangle cutouts, measure up 5½″ from the bottom end of a leg piece along the centerline and mark. Measure in 3″ along the bottom of the piece from each bottom corner and mark. Draw straight lines connecting these marks, forming a triangle (Figure 8-5, lines *c*). Repeat for the other leg.

Place a centered line (about 4″ long) across the centerline 7″ from the bottom of each leg piece (Figure 8-5, line *d*). This is the stretcher placement line.

For the heart cutout, place a mark on the centerline 8½″ from the bottom of each leg piece (Figure 8-5, line *e*). Center the heart pattern (page 148) on the centerline, with the bottom point of the heart at the 8½″ mark; transfer the pattern to each leg with graphite paper.

Reset the saw blade to zero and make all cuts as marked (lines *b* and *c* and heart *e* on Figure 8-5). To ensure greater control, clamp the leg piece you're cutting to your worktable. Check the accuracy of your cuts by standing the legs up together; the cuts should match exactly. Plane or rasp as needed.

3. To round the lower ends of each 1″ x 6″ x 48″ apron, position a 1-quart can on each lower corner and draw a quarter circle (Figure 8-6). Cut off the corners with a saber saw. To provide alignment marks for the legs, measure and mark the top edge of the apron 2¾″ from each end. Mark the other apron the same way.

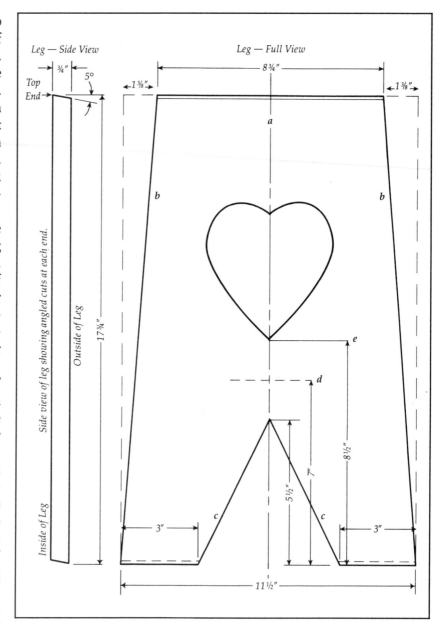

FIG. 8-5. *Leg of country bench, two views.*

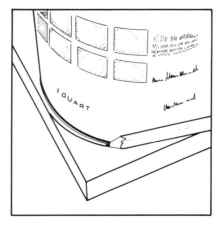

FIG. 8-6. *Draw a quarter circle at each lower corner.*

4. Once again, set the saw blade at a 5-degree angle and cut the stretcher to a length of 43⅜″ from the 1″ x 3″ x 48″ piece. Cuts are made at both ends, but on this piece, cut from opposite sides of the board to produce opposite slopes. To help in centering this piece during assembly, draw a short centerline at each end on the "long" (43⅜″) side of the board (the other side will measure about 43¼″).

5. Sand all pieces thoroughly, taking care not to remove the alignment marks.

PUTTING IT TOGETHER

1. To attach the aprons to the legs, place one leg piece on its side and position one end of an apron on the leg. The alignment mark on the apron must be even with the outside edge of the leg, top edges flush. (NOTE: The *outside* top edge of the apron must be flush with the top edge of the leg. Otherwise, the outside edge of the apron will interfere with the placement of the seat. See Figure 8-7.) Position an 8d nail ¾" from the top of the apron (Figure 8-8) and drive the nail through the apron into the leg. (Only one of the three nails is used at this time; the remaining nails will be driven after the stretcher has been installed.) Attach the other leg to the other end of the apron. Supporting the legs, turn the bench over and attach the other apron in the same way.

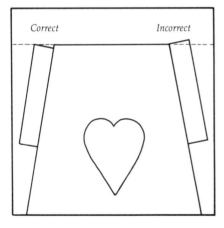

FIG. 8-7. *The outside edge of the apron should be flush with the top edge of the leg.*

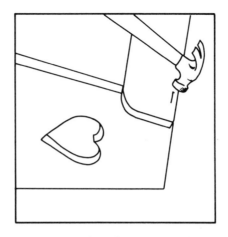

FIG. 8-8. *Attaching the apron to the legs.*

2. To attach the stretcher, carefully stand the bench on end and position the stretcher between the legs (Figure 8-9). Align the center of one end of the stretcher on the stretcher placement line and centerline and drive three evenly spaced 8d nails through the leg and into the stretcher. Carefully turn the assembly over onto the other end; align and nail the other leg to the stretcher in the same way.

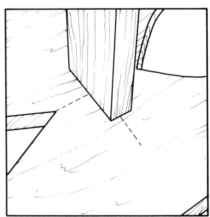

FIG. 8-9. *Attaching the stretcher.*

3. Rest the bench on its side. Adjust the legs so that they are at equal angles to the apron. When they are evenly positioned, drive two more evenly spaced nails through the top apron into each leg. Turn the bench over and drive two more nails into *one* leg only, leaving the other free to allow for leveling of the feet if necessary.

4. Set the bench on the floor. If one foot does not rest on the floor, press the leg either inward or outward to adjust it and drive in the last two nails. This step can help to compensate for unevenness due to slight warpage or minor inaccuracies in cutting.

5. Center the 1" x 12" x 48" seat on the bench, ends flush. Use ten 8d nails to secure the seat, all spaced about 1" from the edge: place one nail about 2" from each end on each side, and the remaining six equally spaced, three on each side.

FINISHING

1. Countersink all the nails and fill the nail holes with wood filler. Sand the wood filler flush when dry. Round the corners and edges of the bench with a rasp or plane.

2. For an added decorative touch after painting or staining, you might want to stencil a design along the aprons.

Trestle Table

THE EARLIEST known American trestle tables date from the mid-seventeenth century. The tops on these tables were often fashioned from a single board, sometimes measuring up to 12′ long and 30″ wide. Our version of this traditional country-style table would make an attractive addition to your kitchen or dining room, and it is relatively easy to make. Standard dimensions of pine boards are used, so the time involved in constructing this project is minimal. Besides being easy to make, it is an inexpensive project: if you use No. 2 pine, the total cost — including finishing — should be less than $50. And since you might want it to mimic a time-worn country piece with all the inherent imperfections, there's no need to spend a great deal of time on the finishing process. Instead, try some of the antiquing techniques described in Chapter 1 (page 20).

Why not get started — you'll be surprised at how soon it's done. Before you know it, you and yours will be gathered around this table, and everyone will be toasting you for your Yankee ingenuity (and frugality!).

SUPPLIES
Two 1″ x 12″ x 48″ pieces of pine
Four 1″ x 3″ x 72″ pieces of pine
Three 1″ x 10″ x 48″ pieces of pine
Two 1″ x 2″ x 72″ pieces of pine
Tape measure, yardstick, pencil
Saber saw
1-quart paint can or 1-pound coffee can
Combination or framing square
Sandpaper (medium and fine)
Wood glue
Two C-clamps
Drill with a No. 10 flat-head counterbore bit
Twenty 1½″ No. 10, four 1¼″ No. 10, and four 3″ No. 10 flat-head wood screws
Medium flat-tipped screwdriver
Twenty 8d finishing nails, hammer
Rasp or plane
Wood filler
Tack cloth
Four ⁵⁄₁₆″ wooden round-top buttons
Paint or stain

LAYING OUT AND CUTTING THE PIECES
(Refer to Figure 8-10)

NOTE: There will be minor variations in the finished width of standard dimension lumber. To compensate for this, the measurements used in this project are given as a distance from the edge; you need only be concerned with the accurate length of the pieces and the squareness of the cuts.

1. Cut two 1″ x 12″ x 28¼″ pieces for the legs (A), being certain that the cuts are square. At the top end of each piece, measure in 2¼″ from each side and mark. From each mark draw a straight line to the same-side corner at the bottom end. Draw a vertical centerline on each leg piece and extend this line over the top edge. (The side you mark on will be the inside of the leg.) To establish the stretcher and heart placement

Detail from color plate 3.

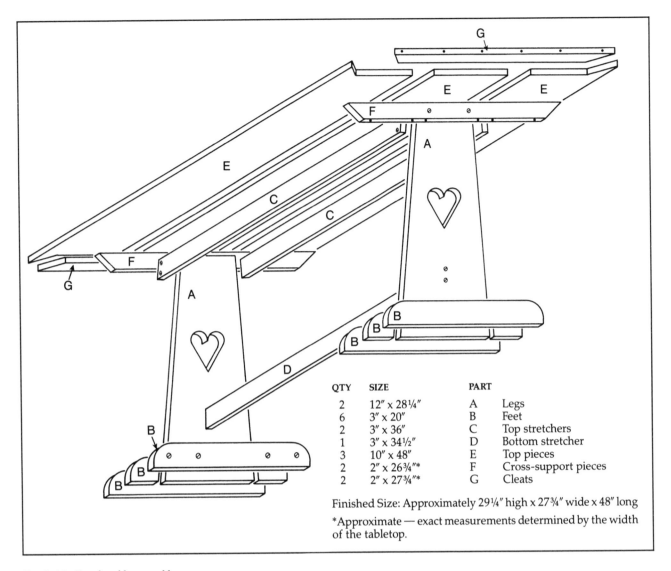

QTY	SIZE	PART	
2	12″ x 28¼″	A	Legs
6	3″ x 20″	B	Feet
2	3″ x 36″	C	Top stretchers
1	3″ x 34½″	D	Bottom stretcher
3	10″ x 48″	E	Top pieces
2	2″ x 26¾″*	F	Cross-support pieces
2	2″ x 27¾″*	G	Cleats

Finished Size: Approximately 29¼″ high x 27¾″ wide x 48″ long

*Approximate — exact measurements determined by the width of the tabletop.

FIG. 8-10. *Trestle table assembly.*

points, measure from the bottom along this centerline on each leg piece, and mark at 6½″ and 9½″ for the stretcher; 7½″ and 8½″ for the screw holes; and 13½″ for the heart. Place the bottom point of the heart pattern (page 155) at the 13½″ mark, center it, and trace it. Cut the sides of the legs and the hearts. (See the bottom of page 141 for tips on cutting out the heart.)

2. Cut six 20″ lengths of 1″ x 3″ for the feet (B) (use only two of the 1″ x 3″ pieces for this). Using a 1-quart paint can (with the outside edge of the can aligned on one end), draw an arc to round one corner; repeat at the other end on the same side of the board. Cut arcs on both ends of all six pieces. Use a square to draw a centerline across the width of one piece and extend this line over the top edge. Hold one leg vertically on a flat surface and match the centerline of the marked foot with the leg centerline. Draw a line on the foot piece on each side of the leg. Cut along these lines, discarding the center part of the foot piece. Repeat these steps with one foot piece only for the other leg. These will be the center foot pieces (of three) for each leg.

3. From the 1″ x 3″ pieces cut two 36″-long top stretchers (C) and one 34½″-long bottom stretcher (D).

4. The top (E) is made of three 1″ x 10″ x 48″ pieces set side by side. The cuts for the cleats (G) are made after the top is assembled. Measure the combined width of the three top pieces. Miter cut both ends of two pieces of 1″ x 2″ pine to a length 1″ shorter than this measurement (approximately 26¾″). These are the cross-support pieces (F).

5. Sand all pieces thoroughly.

PUTTING IT TOGETHER

1. Hold a leg upright on a smooth, level surface. Spread wood glue evenly on *both* sides of the two small center foot pieces and on the inner sides of the other two foot pieces for this leg. Flank the leg with the four foot pieces, aligning them at both ends (be sure to use the foot pieces that were cut for this leg). Before the glue sets, use a square to check that the centerline is perpendicular and reposition if necessary. Clamp the feet at each end, using scraps of wood under the clamp pads to avoid denting the pine. After the pieces have been clamped, drill four counterbored holes along the inside of the whole foot. (See Figure 8-10 for placement.) Check that the counterbore bit is set for 1½" screws; drill the holes deep enough that the screw heads will be recessed ⅜" below the surface of the wood. Drive the screws, then remove the clamps. Repeat for the other leg.

2. Place one leg on its side with the centerline mark facing up. Using a No. 10 counterbore bit (set for 1½" screws), drill both bottom stretcher holes (marks at 7½" and 8½") just through the leg. Turn the leg over and counterbore to a depth of about ³⁄₁₆". Place the leg upright and position one end of the stretcher (D) on the centerline between the placement marks. Push an 8d nail through the holes to mark the drill points on the stretcher end. Turn the stretcher on end and drill to a depth of about ¾" at these points. Repeat for the other leg. Then spread glue on the stretcher ends and attach the stretcher to the legs with 3" No. 10 screws.

3. Carefully turn the leg assembly on its side again. Position the top of one top stretcher (C) even with the top of each leg, ends flush. Use two 8d finishing nails, spaced ⅝" from the top and bottom and ⅜" from the end, to attach the piece. (You may substitute 1½" screws if your ability to drive a nail accurately is a little rusty or if there are knots where the nails will fall.) Attach the other end of the stretcher to the other leg, then turn the assembly over and attach the remaining stretcher.

4. Place the top pieces (E) on a flat surface, tops facing down. Near both ends, measure and mark the center of the total width and draw a centerline from end to end. To determine the placement of the first cross-support piece (F), measure 6" from one end of the top and draw a line across the total width. Mark the midpoint of the cross support and draw a line across the 2" width. Center this piece just *outside* the 6" line. Mark a drill point on this piece ¾" from each end on the bottom edge. Then mark four more drill holes, each approximately 1" from the inside edge of a top board. (You're going to drill from the bottom edge of the cross-support piece into the tabletop, 1" from each inside edge of a top board. See Figure 8-11.) With the counterbore bit

set for 1½" screws, drill centered, ½" counterbored holes at these points through the cross support and into the top. Drive all screws, then carefully place the leg assembly upside down on the top, next to the cross support. Draw a centerline across the other cross-support piece and center it just outside the other leg and, using it as a guide, mark the top. Remove the leg assembly, drill the holes just as you did for the first side, and attach the other cross support.

5. With the leg assembly right side up, place the top on the leg assembly and maneuver it until the top centerline matches the leg centerlines. Set the counterbore bit for 1¼" screws and drill two countersunk holes 1" from each leg edge through the cross support (F) and into the leg. (See Figure 8-10 for placement.) Drive the screws to secure the top to the legs. Repeat on the other side.

6. To make the cleats (G), cut one piece of 1" x 2" pine to the exact width of the tabletop. Miter cut each end with opposing 45-degree angles. To use this piece as a pattern for the recess in the tabletop (see Figure 8-10), clamp it onto one end of the tabletop, aligning its longer side along the tabletop end. Draw a line on the tabletop around this piece, remove the piece, and carefully saw out the

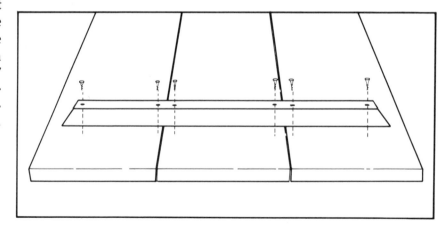

FIG. 8-11. *Drill holes for the cross-support piece.*

recess in the tabletop. Fit the cleat into this recess and attach it with six 8d finishing nails, two in each top board. (See Figure 8-10.) Adjust the tabletop boards as necessary while driving the nails to help level the top. Repeat this process for the other end of the table.

FINISHING

1. Sand the top until it is smooth. Round the edges and corners with a plane or rasp. Countersink the nails on the edge of the tabletop and fill the holes with wood filler. Sand the filler flush when it is dry. Wipe with a tack cloth.

2. Tap a wooden button into each bottom-stretcher screw hole in the legs. They should fit tightly, but apply glue if necessary.

3. This piece looks nice either painted or stained.

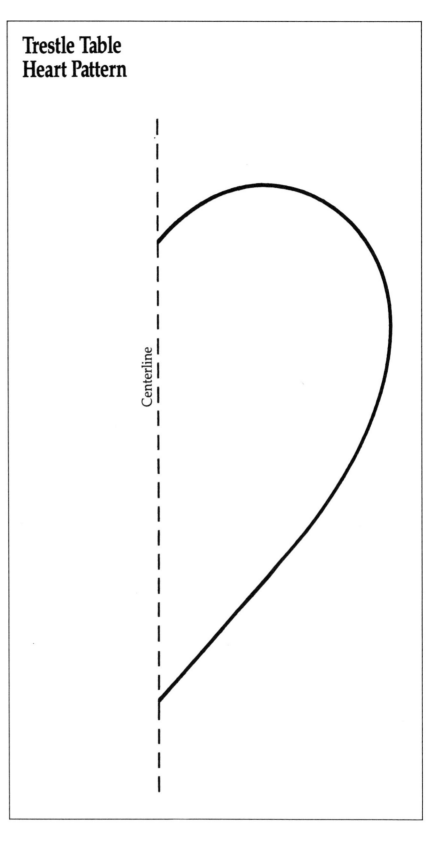

**Trestle Table
Heart Pattern**

Centerline

Glossary

Basecoat: To apply one or more coats of paint to cover an area. When basecoating a large surface (such as a checkerboard), apply two or three thin coats, painting with the direction of the grain.

Bridges: Necessary separations between design cutouts on a stencil.

Color-separated stencil: A separate stencil for each color of the design.

Counterbore: To drill a shallow hole slightly larger than the diameter of the screw head so that the screw head can be recessed below the surface of the wood. The diameter and depth of the hole are determined by the size of the plug or button used to conceal the screw head.

Counterbore bit: A drill bit designed to make either countersink or counterbore holes for screws. These bits come in sizes that correspond to standard screw sizes.

Countersink: To form a funnel-shaped enlargement at the outer end of a drilled hole so that a flat-head wood screw will be flush with the surface when inserted. Also, to drive a nail head below the surface of the wood to conceal it.

Countersink bit: A drill bit designed to make countersink enlargements in drilled holes.

Dead knot: A knot found in lumber which is characterized by a dark brown ring and is the result of live wood growing around a dead branch. It is likely to fall out, as it will shrink with the passage of time. Avoid dead knots in your selection of lumber.

Dry-brush technique: Painting or stenciling using a brush that has been blotted almost dry on a paper towel. This technique will give a delicate, powdery look to the painted surface.

Extender: A liquid used to thin and blend acrylic paint without diluting the color intensity. When extender is mixed with the paint, the drying time is slightly increased.

Feathering: Light, wispy painting strokes made with a dry and worn natural-bristle brush (the bristles should be splayed for best results). This is a good technique for painting fur and feathers on a design (such as the kittens in Chapter 5 or the decoy in Chapter 7).

Full-design stencil: A stencil that incorporates all the elements of a design.

Graphite paper: A graphite-covered paper used for transferring patterns and designs; similar to carbon paper.

Highlight: To apply a light color to accent and bring out an area of a design where the most light would fall.

Knot: A natural imperfection in lumber, a section of a branch that had been growing out of the log from which the board was cut. Both live and dead knots will be present in all but the highest grade (clear) lumber. See *Live knot* and *Dead knot* in this glossary.

Lattice: Long (8') pieces of ¼" clear pine found in the molding section of hardware stores; it is available in various widths.

Live knot: Characterized by its orangish color, a live knot is dense and brittle and should not be used where it will be nailed, screwed, or cut.

Miter: A joint made by cutting two pieces of wood, canvas, or other material at complementary angles and then fitting the cut edges together. A miter cut is a 45-degree-angle cut.

Mylar: A trade name for the acetate used to make stencils. Available in sheets at art or drafting supply stores. Use medium-weight, frosted-on-one-side Mylar; the frosted side takes pen and pencil marks well.

Nominal measurement: In lumber, the pre-planed measurement by which a piece of wood is referred to, even though the wood has been planed and is smaller as a result. True of width and thickness measurements only.

Orrisroot: A substance derived from the root of the Florentine iris plant that can be used as a fixative of the fragrance in potpourri. It is available in powdered or ground form from herb-craft dealers.

Pitch: Sticky, yellow resin found in pine wood. Avoid buying wood in which it is present.

Reach: The part of a wagon that extends from the front axle to the handle.

Rip cut: A cut made parallel to the grain of the wood. To make such a cut.

Running stitch: A series of small, evenly sized and spaced stitches.

Spade bit: A wide, flat drill bit used for boring holes larger than the capacity of the drill chuck.

Stylus: A metal or wooden blunt-tipped instrument (resembling a pen) used in this book for tracing patterns, painting dots, and sculpting pierced lampshades. Available at art supply stores.

Tack cloth: A sticky varnish-coated cheesecloth used to pick up and hold dust from wood after sanding or before finishing.

Tracing paper: Transparent paper used for tracing patterns. Sold in pads or sheets at stationery and art supply stores.

Source Guide

THE COMPANIES listed below will send information and prices to you upon request. Mail a postcard asking for an up-to-date price list or catalog (there may be a fee for some catalogs).

Art Supplies

Dick Blick
P.O. Box 1267
Galesburg, IL 61401

Cornhusks

The Corn Crib
Dept. CW 12, R.R. 2
Box 109
Madison, MO 65263

Herbs and Dried Flowers

Tom Thumb Workshops
P.O. Box 332
Chincoteague, VA 23336

Well-Sweep Herb Farm
317 Mount Bethel Road
Port Murray, NJ 07865

Lamp Supplies

The Lamp Shop
54 South Main Street
Box 36
Concord, NH 03301

Metal Wheels

Harmony Products
P.O. Box 16543
Winston-Salem, NC 27115

Milk Paint

Old-Fashioned Milk Paint Company
Box 222
Groton, MA 01450

Saw Blades, Drill Bits

The Olson Saw Company
Rt. 6, Stony Hill
Bethel, CT 06801

Seeds and Gardening Supplies

W. Atlee Burpee
Warminster, PA 18974

Wood and Woodworking Supplies

Albert Constantine
2050 Eastchester Road
Bronx, NY 10461

Van Dyke Supply Company
P.O. Box 278
4th Avenue and 6th Street
Woonsocket, SD 57385

Books You Will Enjoy

American Country Furniture, 1780–1875 by Ralph and Terry Kovel. New York: Clarkson N. Potter/Publishers, 1965.

American Folk Art Designs & Motifs for Artists & Craftspeople by Joseph D'Addetta. New York: Dover Publications, 1984.

American Folk Art in Wood, Metal and Stone by Jean Lipman. New York: Dover Publications, 1972.

American Wildfowl Decoys by Jeff Waingrow. New York: E.P. Dutton, 1985.

Antiques of American Childhood by Katherine Morrison McClinton. New York: Clarkson N. Potter/Publishers, 1970.

Collecting American Country by Mary Ellisor Emmerling. New York: Clarkson N. Potter/Publishers, 1983.

Early American Stencils on Walls and Furniture by Janet Waring. New York: Dover Publications, 1968.

The Flowering of American Folk Art (1776–1876) by Jean Lipman and Alice Winchester. Philadelphia: Courage Books, 1987.

Folk Art Motifs of Pennsylvania by Frances Lichten. New York: Dover Publications, 1976.

A Gallery of American Weathervanes and Whirligigs by Robert Bishop and Patricia Coblentz. New York: E.P. Dutton, 1981.

Gameboards of North America by Bruce and Doranna Wendel. New York: E.P. Dutton, 1986.

Herbs — Gardens, Decorations, and Recipes by Emelie Tolley and Chris Mead. New York: Clarkson N. Potter/ Publishers, 1985.

Herbs — How to Select, Grow and Enjoy by Norma Jean Lathrop. Tucson: HP Books, 1981.

An Introduction to 21 Traditional Yankee Home Crafts by Barbara Radcliffe Rogers. Dublin, New Hampshire: Yankee, Inc., 1979.

Techniques in American Folk Decoration by Jean Lipman. New York: Dover Publications, 1972.

1001 Designs for Whittling & Woodcarving by E.J. Tangerman. New York: Bonanza Books, 1979.